THE DAY THEY FELL FROM THE SKY

10 LONE SURVIVORS AND THEIR HARROWING AND INCREDIBLE TRUE STORIES OF PLANE-CRASH SURVIVAL

OLIVER MARTIN CASS

To my lovely daughters Sophia and Olivia, you are my treasure and inspiration.

And to my soulmate, best friend, and wife, Kazia. I love you with all my heart.

CONTENTS

INTRODUCTION

Since the dawn of time, humans have survived insurmountable odds stacked against them. From wars to pandemics to natural disasters, people have evolved to survive and thrive throughout time. Over the course of history, personal stories of tragedies and disasters have always given us a sense of curiosity and fascination as to human perseverance and the will to survive. Even during modern times, you often hear about people surviving getting lost at sea, being marooned, or even lost in a forest. What you don't always hear about are those who manage to survive a plane crash.

Many people are terrified of flying. Their main reasons are generally the sheer height and possibility of a crash. The general assumption about plane crashes is that when one occurs, every single person dies horribly. Some people are so scared of flying that they would rather drive for multiple, extra hours or even days to get to their destination. They believe that driving is safer than flying. This is a long-standing belief that is highly inaccurate.

In 2018, the number of fatal plane crashes was one in 16 million flights, while fatal car crashes was one in 114 trips (Lesser

Lesser Landy & Smith PLLC, 2021). That said, these fatal plane crashes were only for flights governed by the Federal Aviation Administration (FAA) regulation 14 Code of Federal Regulations (CFR) Part 121. These are only planes that fly for commercial usage and are heavily regulated by federal law. Planes under this regulation have strict standards when it comes to pilot training, maintenance, and inspections. However, not all planes are governed by this regulation.

Certifications and operations for planes with a capacity of 20 or more are regulated by 14 CFR Part 125, while chartered or on-demand planes are regulated by 14 CFR Part 135. Even privately-owned planes are governed by a different regulation (14 CFR Part 91 for general aviation). These smaller planes generally have a lower standard of regulations than those used for commercial flying. Therefore, the requirements surrounding maintenance, inspections, and pilot training and retraining are often not to the same standards as those applied to commercial planes.

In 2021, the United Nations reported over 1.3 million deaths caused by road accidents and over 50 million injuries worldwide (United Nations News, 2021). When compared to fatal plane crashes of the same year, there were only 15 fatal aircraft accidents (Learmount, 2022). This resulted in 134 deaths, of which only one fatal crash was from a commercial plane. On January 9, 2021, Sriwijaya Air Flight 182 (Boeing 737-500) crashed soon after taking off, killing all 62 passengers on board. The remainder of the accidents were from planes not covered by 14 CFR Part 121. If that wasn't enough evidence of commercial plane safety, in 2020, there were only 12 fatal accidents resulting in 332 deaths and 22 fatal accidents in 2019, resulting in 297 deaths. Each year, there are consistently fewer deaths resulting from flying. So, in essence, commercial flying is far safer than driving a car.

Yet people are still terrified to fly. Why? When a car crashes, there are a handful of deaths on average. When a plane crashes, there are significantly more deaths that result from only one incident. Plane crashes can be gruesome, as they cause devastation to the area around the crash sites, people's lives (suitcases, clothes, etc.) lie bare for the world to see, and sometimes, there are huge explosions. Even then, despite how horrific the scenes of a plane crash are, some people manage to live through the tragedy.

The first commercial flight—one that contained a paying passenger—was on January 01, 1914. It was a short flight of only 23 minutes, from St. Petersburg to Tampa, Florida. The trip was only 17 miles, but saved a lot of travel time compared to traveling by railway or car. The pilot was Tony Jannus, the passenger was Abram C. Pheil, and the ticket had cost $400. Although this business only lasted for four months, it was the start of a trend that would grow into hundreds of airlines throughout the world.

Yet, despite all successes, there were also failures. What has been considered the first commercial plane crash was on December 14, 1920. It was a British Handley Page HP-16 traveling from London to Paris. Sadly, it crashed soon after takeoff, killing four of the eight people on board at the time.

According to the Bureau of Aircraft Accidents Archives (B3A), there have been over 28,000 plane crashes from 1918 up until early 2022 (Bureau of Aircraft Accidents Archives, n.d.-a). The planes included in these crashes are those that carried more than six people and excluded vehicles such as helicopters, gliders, balloons, and fighter planes. Any military planes included in this list are those not in active combat (troop transports, reconnaissance missions, etc.) and had to have the capacity to carry more than six people. Another factor used to include accidents in this list is that the planes were written off or destroyed after the incident that caused the crash. Because of this, there is the likelihood that there have been more crashes that have not been fully documented.

From these crashes listed by the B3A, over 158,000 people were lost due to impact wounds, burns, smoke inhalation, and other injuries sustained during the accident. The B3A has determined that the worst years to fly were 1943–1945, with 815, 945, and 737 crashes, respectively (Bureau of Aircraft Accidents Archives, n.d.-b). This resulted in 4,060, 4,647, and 4,700 deaths from 1943–1945, respectively (Bureau of Aircraft Accidents Archives, n.d.-c). As time progressed, there were fewer accidents, but now and again, there would be peaks in mishaps and deaths. These would be dependent on many factors from lack of training, pilot error, structural faults, etc.

Although it is possible to calculate the number of people who survived accidents when looking at individual crashes, there is no detailed list of who managed to walk away from these gruesome accidents. Survivors are rarely tracked for future reference. So, what happens to these people? They tend to become a story, milled over by millions who read about the accidents. Sometimes their lives are ruled by the accident, and this leads them to struggle to escape the stigma behind the crash. This is especially true if the survivor is a pilot and the investigation reveals the crash was caused by pilot error. Other times, they fade into obscurity, hoping to never have to come face-to-face with what may have scarred them not only physically, but mentally and emotionally, too. All are affected by the loss and guilt they are forced to carry through no fault of their own.

SURVIVOR'S GUILT

Something that many survivors suffer from is survivor's guilt. Whether it's a soldier, a car crash victim, or the sole survivor of a plane crash, they all feel a pang of guilt at having lived when others did not. This is considered one of the symptoms of post-traumatic stress disorder (PTSD), although not everyone who suffers from PTSD has survivor's guilt.

Common emotional symptoms which develop are helplessness,

anxiety, depression, and even thoughts of suicide. Some physical symptoms include stomach aches, insomnia, a racing heart rate, flashbacks, and even nightmares.

The most common phrase uttered by survivors is, "Why me?", and sadly, it is difficult to answer, if even at all. Survivor's guilt has a negative impact on the individual. They may have to go through years of therapy and medication to help deal with the guilt over something that they had no control over.

ABOUT THE AUTHOR

My name is Oliver Martin Cass, and I'm from stunning New Zealand. Here, I live with my wife and two children. I have always been an avid reader. Because of this, I developed a passion for writing, starting with my personal blog and then developing content for the family business.

Stories of survival, in particular, have touched me deeply ever since I was a child. My father, a cargo ship captain, nearly lost his life after his ship sank off the coast of the northern Philippines, and luckily, he escaped with his entire crew. Since then, I have always been intrigued and inspired by those who made it through tragedy and adversity. I'm curious what sets survivors apart from many who have lost hope and succumbed to life's greatest challenges.

In this book, I have collected the stories of 10 extraordinary people who survived what many perceive as impossible. Not only did these seemingly ordinary men, women, and children survive a plane crash, they were the *only survivors*. It is exponentially rare for there to only be one survivor from a crash of a large commercial plane, but it isn't unheard of. These 10 people are just part of a very small group, but they aren't alone. How did these individuals make it through such extraordinary circumstances? Did they have special skills, or was it all down to luck? Would you have done what they did? Or would you succumb to despair, giving up all hope? Would you strive with all your might to live and fight to see another day?

Read on to discover these survivors' extraordinary journeys from the day of their accidents, to the subsequent investigations, to how their lives have turned out, for better or worse. By the end of the book, you will have a deeper understanding of what the survivors have gone through and how they used it to live their lives. As a bonus chapter, some tips will be revealed that may help improve your chances of survival if you ever find yourself in similar conditions.

DISCLAIMER

All the facts listed in this book are based on the reports and interviews of those involved in the crashes or investigations which followed. It is not this book's intent to blame anyone for what happened, but rather, to state facts and observations which came to light after investigations were completed. The only intent of this book is to educate. My heart goes out to those affected by these tragedies, be they ground crew, survivors, families of the deceased, and anyone else caught up in the accidents.

1

BAHIA BAKARI: THE "MIRACLE GIRL" FROM FRANCE

I was hearing people speak but I couldn't see anyone. I was in the dark. I couldn't see anything. –Bahia Bakari

Bahia Bakari was born on August 15, 1996 in Évry, Essonne, close to Paris, to mother, Aziza Aboudou, and father, Kassim Bakari. She was the oldest of four children with two younger brothers, Badru and Badavi, and a little sister, Badyan. Although she was French from birth, her parents were originally from the Comoros Islands. For 12 years, Bahia had an average childhood, until June 30, 2009. What was meant to be a family reunion between Bahia and her mother with family in Comoros soon turned into a nightmare.

THE DAY SHE FELL FROM THE SKY

Bahia and her mother were traveling from Paris, France to Moroni, Comoros (between Tanzania and Madagascar) to visit some family during the summer vacation. Their flight was broken into four parts, and they were in the final stage, traveling from Sana'a, Yemen to Moroni. Yemenia Flight 626 (Airbus A310-324) contained 142 passengers and 11 crew members. It had been an uneventful flight until seven minutes before landing. Instead of making the final turn to head toward the runway, the plane went off course, stalled, and then dropped from the sky into the Indian Ocean. The control tower at Prince Said Ibrahim International Airport knew the flight was inbound, but lost communication soon after it had crashed into the ocean at about 1:30 a.m. local time (22:50 UTC). It was dark, and the weather was poor. At its strongest, the wind was blowing at 38 mph.

Yet Bahia was unaware of this. The last thing she remembered was being told that they were going to crash and needed to fasten their seat belts as the plane started to go down. Then, her memory mercifully faded away until she was awoken by what she described as an electrical shock. She was surrounded by darkness and churning waters. She wasn't a good swimmer and scrambled to find something, anything, to hang onto to prevent the waves from swallowing her. She was just barely keeping afloat on a piece of the fuselage as she had no life vest.

Bahia had no idea what had happened, and at first thought she had been sucked out of the plane because she had pressed up against the window too hard. She thought that this had happened because she hadn't worn a seat belt. She didn't know she had just survived a plane crash.

In the surrounding dark, she could hear voices and even some women crying, but she couldn't see them. Although she had survived the initial crash, she was at the mercy of the elements and the ocean. One by one, the voices around her were swallowed until she was left all alone, floating among bodies and debris. Here, the young girl would float for over nine hours before help arrived.

The ship *Sima Com 2* was the first boat of those that volunteered to scour the ocean for possible survivors. It came across Bahia about nine miles from the closest Comoros coastline. The crew members hoped that they would find someone alive, but soon realized that the crash had caused the plane to be torn apart, and there was a slim chance anyone would survive that. Slim, but not impossible. Thankfully, they spotted Bahia among the wreckage and threw her a life buoy. However, after a plane crash, being assaulted by the Indian Ocean for over nine hours, and the waves still battering her, Bahia was exhausted. She had all but given up when the rescuers had called to her to come to them.

She let go of the debris she had clung to overnight, and immediately, a wave submerged her. Using what strength she had left, she managed to surface. However, the rescuers knew that she was too weak to reach the life buoy. One rescuer, Libouna Sélémani Matrafi, didn't hesitate for a second. He dove into the water and swam 100 feet out to the terrified and exhausted child. She clung to him as he made his way back to the life buoy. The remainder of the rescuers pulled the two of them aboard the ship before they wrapped Bahia in some dry blankets and gave her some warm sugar water to drink. From what they could see, she was suffering from hypothermia and shock. Once hospitalized, it was found that she was suffering from a fractured collarbone. This was the worst of her injuries. Others noted were the bruising to her face, elbow, and foot, as well as some burns.

Meanwhile, her father, having heard of the plane crash, was devastated that he had lost his wife and eldest daughter. He initially thought of his daughter as fragile and not having the ability to survive such a tragedy. Yet, deep down, he still held out hope that by some miracle his family would make it through. Once he heard his daughter had survived against all the odds, he marveled at the inner strength Bahia must have drawn on to survive. She had survived a plane crash, been alone overnight in the Indian Ocean, and had minimal injuries.

At this stage, Bahia was very weak and could barely answer any questions other than gesturing or giving single-word answers. She had to be convinced that she had not been sucked out of the plane, but rather, in a plane crash. Once she was physically strong enough, she was sent back to France before spending some time recovering in the Armand-Trousseau Children's Hospital. While she was on Comoros, no one had told her what had happened to her mother. She had been under the impression that she was just in the next room, recovering. However, this was not the case, and eventually, this news had to be broken to her. She was the sole survivor of 153 passengers on board Yemenia Flight 626. For surviving against all odds, Bahia Bakari was dubbed *"La Miraculée"* ("The Miracle Girl"). She sent a message to the world that just about anything was possible.

FATAL DISTRACTION: WHY FLIGHT 626 FELL

It is rare that the cause of a crash (fatal or otherwise) is unknown, and it didn't take long to figure out what happened to Yemenia Flight 626. It was determined after an investigation that the crash was the result of incorrect actions taken by the crew on the flight controls, which caused an aerodynamic stall.

An "aerodynamic stall" occurs when the airflow of the wings of a plane is disturbed in some way. This causes a loss of lift and an increase in air resistance. Usually, this occurs during takeoff and landing, as the plane starts to reduce speed. At lower speeds, the aerodynamic forces are also reduced, lowering the forces of lift. The pilot (or copilot) compensates for this by increasing the angle of attack.

The "angle of attack" is an angle created between the oncoming (relative) wind and the reference (cord) line of the plane's wing. When the speed is too low, there is a chance that the angle of attack reaches a critical level, which once exceeded, can cause the plane to stall. There is the possibility that a stalled plane *can* recover, but this is not always the case.

It was believed that those at the flight controls weren't paying attention to the angle of attack, and this caused the plane to stall and drop from the sky. For some reason, they were not able to correct it before the plane plummeted into the Indian Ocean.

On a side note, Airbus A310-324 wasn't a plane usually used by the French, as it had failed an aviation inspection in 2007. This is why the plane was no longer seen in France. However, Yemenia Airlines still used the plane, and the one involved in the crash was 19 years old. This disaster almost caused the European Union to blacklist flights from Yemenia. This incident exposed a problem that hadn't been brought to light before: are older plane models being made fit to fly according to worldwide standardized aircraft maintenance?

BAHIA'S LIFE MOVES FORWARD

According to the Aviation Safety Network, Bahia became the first sole survivor of the deadliest crash into an ocean. A record none, thankfully, has taken from her. She is also the second person to sole-survive the deadliest plane crash. That so-called 'honor' belongs to Cecelia Cichan, who will be discussed later. In 2010, Bahia released a book titled *Moi Bahia, la miraculée* (*I'm Bahia, the miracle girl*), alongside Omar Guendouz, explaining what she went through. Despite writing this book, her father stated that she sometimes closes herself off from others.

This is understandable, seeing as it is difficult for survivors to talk to non-survivors about what they lived through. People may say they understand, but they don't really until they experience the horror themselves.

In 2013, a documentary called *Sole Survivor*, by writer-director Ky Dickens, starred four sole survivors who came together to talk about what had happened to them. Alongside Bahia were Cecelia Cichan (known as "The Toddler"), George Lamson Jr. ("The Seeker"), and James 'Jim' Polehinke ("The Copilot"). All of these people were those who had managed to survive horrific plane crashes, which left them the only survivors. With these guests, Bahia revisited the devastation she went through to try and heal from the trauma. This trauma is something that never goes away, and survivors need to deal with it until the end of their lives.

There have only been 14 sole survivors from commercial plane crashes since 1970. Of the survivors, about a third were either children or cabin crew members. This begs the question: do children have a better chance of surviving compared to adults? Unfortunately, there is no clear-cut answer for this, as there are many external factors that can play a role in someone surviving a plane crash.

In the case of children, it comes down to the size of the child. Young toddlers can easily be cocooned by their chairs while older children and adults aren't, as they tend to suffer more from head or limb injuries. However, this isn't true for children who sit on their parents' laps through the use of an extension seat belt. During sudden deceleration, these children's weights are massively increased, and the parents cannot hold onto them. This can cause the child to be thrown from their lap and even bounce around the inside of the plane. Alternatively, the adult's forward motion—when not bracing correctly with a child—can crush the infant.

Another point is that a lighter body weight in a chair allows the fall to be broken easier by objects such as trees. This is only possible if the height of the fall isn't *too much*—as seen with takeoff or landing. Another factor that protects children a little better than adults is that their bones are more flexible and less likely to shatter upon impact, especially the rib cage. As long as the body's tolerance isn't exceeded, the child should survive the initial crash. However, it may be difficult for young ones to survive on their own if no adults are around to help them afterwards. Another disadvantage children have is that they have thinner skin, making them more susceptible to getting burned. Although children may have a slight advantage over adults, it comes down to too many deciding factors that are beyond everyone's control.

2

LETHAL LIMITS: VESNA VULOVIC'S RECORD-BREAKING STORY

To die is pure destiny—in a plane or, in a car crash, or in the street. The funny thing is that, if you have to die the easiest way to do so is in a plane. So that's it, it wasn't my day for dying. –Vesna Vulović

Vesna Vulovic was born in Belgrade, Serbia, on January 3, 1950, to a mother who was a gym instructor and a father who was a company director. She continued to stay there until she completed her first year at university before deciding to go to London. This decision was two-fold: she wanted to improve her English speaking skills and had a love for The Beatles. The latter drove her passion to travel. She wasn't in London for very long before she returned to Belgrade. It was during this time that she met with a friend who was working for Jat Airways (JAT) Yugoslav Airline. She took one look at the turquoise uniform and was mesmerized. As a flight attendant, she could travel the world and go to many places she had never been to before. This would be the job of a lifetime, and she was right. She became a JAT Yugoslav Airline air stewardess in 1971. It was hard work, but she got to see the world and explore it. She worked with the airline for eight months with no problems. That was until January 26, 1972, when she formed part of the secondary crew of JAT Yugoslav Airlines Flight 367 (McDonnell Douglas DC-9-32 YU-AHT). It was on this flight that she earned her Guinness World Record... not that she wanted to.

THE DAY SHE FELL FROM THE SKY

Flight 367 was flying from Stockholm, Sweden to Belgarde, with two stopovers; one in Copenhagen, Denmark, and another in Zagreb, Croatia. Vesna joined the flight in Copenhagen, but she was never meant to be on that flight. A different flight attendant, also named 'Vesna', was meant to be there, but due to a mix-up, Vulović worked the flight because she had never been to Denmark. Although Vesna doesn't remember anything from the flight, she did remember a man acting annoyed as he stepped from the plane after it had landed in Copenhagen. This man never returned to the plane. Vesna was suspicious of this but never voiced her concerns. This was the last thing she remembered before she awoke, screaming in agony.

The flight had taken off with no problems, but at 4:01 p.m. (less than an hour into the flight), the black boxes showed that the plane suddenly, and with no warning, dropped from the sky. As the plane had flown toward the Czechoslovakian border (now known as "the Czech Republic"), the East German air traffic controllers handed over control to their Czech counterparts. When the Czech air traffic controllers couldn't communicate with the plane, they let their East German counterparts know. Checking the radar, the East Germans noticed that the flight flew into Czechoslovakian airspace before it vanished from radar.

The flight, which carried five crew members and 23 passengers, broke apart into three sections in midair. Pieces of the plane, baggage, and bodies rained down upon the village of Srbská

Kamenice. This village was close to the East German border. Vesna had been trapped in the tail-end of the plane as it fell to the ground. She had been pinned by the food cart, keeping her within the tail section. Despite falling through the air, which was below freezing, Vesna had somehow managed to survive her ordeal. She had just become a wreckage rider.

When free falling without a parachute, there is almost a 100% chance of a person dying upon landing. But by being a wreckage rider (holding onto wreckage in some manner), you can lower your chance of a fatal impact with the ground by slowing your descent. This, coupled with the slope of the mountain, the trees, and the thick snow, Vesna was cushioned from the impact when the tail-end of the plane hit the ground, therefore preserving her life. These weren't the only things that contributed to her survival.

Vesna was never supposed to have passed her medical evaluation to be an air stewardess. She suffered from very low blood pressure. This should have barred her from being an air stewardess. It would be very dangerous for someone who stood in the cabin during flights to have low blood pressure, as they could suffer from postural hypotension. This could lead to them passing out while standing. It is believed that Vesna was nervous about her medical test, and so she had drank enough coffee to raise her blood pressure. This allowed her to pass her physical. This didn't stop her from having low blood pressure, which ended up saving her life when the tail-end slammed into the ground. Had she had normal blood pressure, the impact would likely have caused her heart to explode. By having a lower-than-normal blood pressure, she only passed out during the fall, resulting in her waking up a short time later to find herself covered in blood, under the body of a colleague, and barefoot as her stiletto heels had come off during the fall—all with no memory of what had happened.

Her cries for help eventually alerted a member of a rescue party named Bruno Honke, a woodsman, to find her, despite the darkness and debris lying everywhere. Bruno had been a World War II medic, and he managed to keep Vesna alive until more help could arrive. Despite surviving the plane breaking apart and a massive 33,000-foot (over six miles) drop, Vesna was seriously injured. She had crushed a couple of vertebrae, broke her pelvis, both legs, several ribs, and had a fractured skull. Doctors would later describe her as a “broken woman”, and few held out hope for her survival, though some thought she was strong enough to pull through.

The next thing Vesna knew, she was waking up in the hospital after a long coma, with her parents beside her. She remembered nothing of what had caused the plane to break apart or her rescue. She had to be given a newspaper article explaining the events. She almost went into shock reading what was being said. The plane had exploded in mid-air because of a bomb. Her mind traveled back to the man who had looked so annoyed in Copenhagen. Was he the culprit? No one was sure, as no arrests had been made.

Vesna had gained celebrity status from her survival, but that wasn’t all. It was suspected that the bomb was placed in the plane by the Croatian terroristic group, Ustaše (Ustasha). Soon, after she was recovered from the crash site, she was placed under a 24-hour police guard. They were worried that the Croatian separatist terrorists would try to finish her off once they learned their plot had failed to kill everyone onboard Flight 367. At 22 years old, Vesna was paralyzed from her hips down. Luckily, this was only temporary, as within a year, she was walking on her own again, despite a limp she would have for the rest of her life. Since she couldn’t remember anything, she didn’t develop any fear of flying, resulting in her wanting to return to her job as soon as she was well enough.

BLOWN UP OR SHOT DOWN: WHAT CAUSED FLIGHT 367'S EXPLOSION?

At the time, it was widely accepted that Flight 367 had been brought down by a bomb hidden in a briefcase. It was also believed that this bomb may have been placed on the plane during the stopover in Copenhagen. However, this could never be proven beyond a shadow of a doubt. Despite this, the blame was squarely placed at the feet of Croatian nationalists, as they had already been carrying out terrorist attacks since 1962, with this violence only ending in 1982. This theory was cemented when someone stating that they were a Croatian nationalist called the Swedish newspaper, *Kvöllspoten*, and claimed responsibility for the bombing. However, this lead seemed to go nowhere, and no arrests, even to this day, have ever been made.

However, in 2009, investigative journalists Peter Hornung-Andersen and Pavel Theiner came up with an alternative theory, which was significantly darker than a terrorist bomb. The two men challenged the bomb theory by stating that Flight 367 was shot down by mistake by the Czechoslovak Air Force. They believe that a Czechoslovak MiG fighter mistook the commercial plane as an enemy aircraft, as it had flown too close to a sensitive military facility, one which supposedly stored nuclear weapons. The Czechoslovak Air Defense may also have been a little jumpy, as both the East German leader, Erich Honecker, and Soviet leader, Leonid Brezhnev, were flying to Prague, the Czech Republic, during the time Flight 367 crashed.

The pair even claimed they had eyewitness testimonies that placed another plane in the area where the doomed flight was to fall. They believed the plane had been shot down at 2,625 feet (half a mile) instead of 33,000 feet, which would prove Vesna's miraculous survival. They went on to explain that the narrative of the bomb and fall from 33,000 feet was a propaganda attempt as the so-called "true incident" was covered up by the secret police to prevent anyone from knowing the truth. Though their theory could be plausible, they had based all their evidence off of circumstantial evidence and unverified theories. It is unlikely the full truth will ever be discovered. Regardless, as Vesna couldn't remember what had happened, she couldn't be challenged on the facts, as she had none.

LIFE AFTERWARD AS A WORLD RECORD-HOLDER

Vesna's life was full after her rise to celebrityhood. As she didn't remember the crash, she had no fear of flying and wanted to return to her job as soon as possible. Despite truly wanting to be an air stewardess again, JAT wasn't willing to have her on any more of their flights. It wasn't that they thought she was a jinx, but rather, they didn't want the public attention she would bring to the airline if she were to fly with them again. She was given a desk job later in 1972. Vesna was now in charge of negotiating freight contracts for the airline. She continued to work for the company for another 18 years.

She would still fly from time to time, but only as a passenger, one who was often recognized and hounded by other passengers who wanted to sit next to her. Perhaps they thought she would be a lucky charm if anything were to happen to the flight. She was also awarded a Guinness World Record in 1985 for surviving the highest free fall (33,330 feet) without a parachute. The record still remains in place to this day, despite the circumstantial evidence presented by Hornung-Andersen and Theiner. There was even a folk song recorded in her honor by Serbia's top recording artist, Miroslav Ilić. It was titled *Vesna stjuardesa* (Vesna the stewardess) in 1972. This wasn't the only honor showered upon her. Six weeks after Bruno rescued her, a granddaughter was born to his family, who was named after Vesna. Vesna would later also become an honorary citizen of Srbská Kamenice. It was, after all, the polite thing to do if someone drops into your life unexpectedly.

Vesna was rather outspoken about her political views, and she used her new stardom to campaign them. She was against nationalism and particularly against Statesman Slobodan Milošević, widely known as the "Butcher of Balkans". Unfortunately, due to her openly trying to convince her coworkers not to vote for Slobodan Milošević, JAT Airlines forced her into early retirement by firing her in 1990. This didn't stop her beliefs, and she continued to be outspoken about her views. She took part in many anti-government protests, but managed to avoid getting arrested. It is believed she was never arrested, as the government was concerned about the possible negative press it would bring if they dared to do so. In 2008, she continued to campaign, this time siding with the Democratic Party of then-president, Boris Tadić.

The year 1990 wasn't a good one for Vesna. In 1977, she married her husband Nikola Breka, a mechanical engineer, after a year of dating. Sadly, the couple never had children, despite trying. This was probably due to the injuries she sustained in the crash. Soon after Vesna was fired from her job, her husband left her. She blamed the divorce on her chain-smoking.

Despite being a well-known person, Vesna never lived her life as a celebrity. She enjoyed spending time by herself. She never counted herself as lucky for surviving the plane crash. She felt that it had actually been a curse. She even felt she had been born in the wrong or bad place. The medical costs had all but bankrupted her parents after they were forced to sell both of their cars to pay the mounting bills.

She was also severely affected by survivor's guilt, oftentimes catching herself crying despite never remembering what had happened on the flight. Instead of seeking therapy to treat it, she turned to religion, which seemed to help her. Eventually, she even grew tired of talking about the fall in general, and by 2016, she was living alone with her three cats with a monthly pension of only €300 (a little more than $300).

After not hearing from her for several days, some friends got a locksmith to open her apartment. Sadly, Vesna had passed away at the age of 66 on December 23, 2016. Vesna had been suffering heart problems for several years before her death, and after an autopsy, it was revealed that it was the cause of her death.

3

EIGHT DAYS ALONE: ANNETTE HERFKENS' SURVIVAL JOURNEY

My head is light. The plants around me are radiant. I do not feel the pain any longer. I am both out of my body and close to my body. I have left, but I am present. –Annette Herfkens

At the age of 31, Annette Herfkens had her entire life in order. She was a Dutch native, a successful banker who worked as a trader in Wall Street, and loved her job. She had studied at Leiden University in Leiden, Netherlands. Here, she had met William 'Pasje' van der Pas—who also became a successful banker—while studying. By their fourth year of studies, she knew she wanted to marry him. They continued to date for 13 years before William moved to Vietnam while she was in Madrid.

After being separated for a few months, Annette decided to go visit William in 1992. She boarded a plane to Ho Chi Minh City, Vietnam to see her fiancé. He was thrilled to have her be with him once more. He took her around the city to show her the sites before wrapping up the evening with an intimate dinner at one of his favorite restaurants. He had planned a surprise, five-day, romantic getaway for the two of them at a coastal resort in Nha

Trang, a city of Vietnam along the South China Sea. Annette was ecstatic; it had been three months since she saw him last, and she was grateful to be close to him again.

On November 14, 1992, William and Annette boarded Vietnam Airlines Flight 474 (Yakovlev Yak-40, registered as VN-A449). This was a small, three-engined jet airplane with a capacity for 32 passengers that had been built by the Soviet Union. Annette took one look at the plane and immediately started feeling claustrophobic. She believed that the plane was too old (16 years) and small. She then tried to convince William to instead drive to the resort. William wouldn't relent, as driving a car to the resort would take several days due to the poorly-maintained roads and dense jungle. They would end up arriving at the resort, before having to turn around and return. He continued to soothe her by telling her that the trip would only be 20 minutes, which was a lie. Believing in her fiancé, Annette boarded the plane and waited for takeoff. The flight had 25 passengers and six crew members in total.

Everything was going well until 50 minutes into the flight. The plane suddenly dropped from the sky but seemed to correct itself. A little shaken, but overall managing to control her emotions, Annette looked over to William to see that he was noticeably concerned. She laughed it off and said that they likely hit an air pocket. Turbulence was nothing new to someone who had flown before. She also heard the sound of accelerating motors. However, when the second dip happened, they both realized that something wasn't right. Suddenly, there was a scream from somewhere in the plane before the interior went dark. A few seconds later, the first impact was felt.

THE DAY SHE FELL FROM THE SKY

The first impact was due to the plane hitting some trees along a ridgeline before it collided with a remote mountain in Vietnam.

This second impact caused the plane to flip upside down. Annette wasn't wearing a seat belt, and the first impact caused her to be thrown from her seat before being bounced around the cabin. During her haphazard flailing, she slipped under a seat, legs first, and was pinned in place when the second impact occurred. It was the second impact that tore the plane into pieces. Annette was unconscious for 4–5 hours before she managed to wake up from the trauma. She was under a seat that contained a dead body. Shocked, she immediately started looking for her fiancé, and she soon found him. The damage to the plane had been so severe that his seat had been completely twisted around to face the opposite direction. Annette had hoped that he had survived the crash as well, but although he had a soft smile on his face, he was incredibly pale. At 36 years old, William had died when his seat belt (not a standard over-the-lap belt) had crushed his ribs into his lungs. He wasn't the only one.

The shock at seeing William dead was so severe, Annette couldn't remember crawling from the plane, but when she became aware again, she found herself outside of the aircraft. Her injuries were severe. She had fractured both hips, collapsed a lung, broken her jaw, had an open fracture in one shin (four inches of bone was sticking out of it), and she had a wound on her chin which revealed part of the jawbone.

Outside, she was joined by a Vietnamese businessman. He, too, was injured, but he took pity on her. During the crash landing, her wrap-around skirt had been torn away. The man managed to retrieve a pair of trousers from his suitcase and gave them to her so that her modesty would be protected. He wasn't the only survivor. She could hear moans of pain coming from inside the plane, but no one else joined them outside. The businessman was a great comfort to her with his words and presence, but soon he became weak, started struggling to breathe, and then, all life left him. Soon even the moans from the plane halted; Annette was now the only survivor. Although she had survived the plane crash, she was now stuck in a jungle with no sign of help coming. She would remain there for the next eight days.

She stayed where she was until she could no longer look at the man decaying next to her. With the extent of her injuries, she couldn't walk and would have to drag herself around by her elbows. It was agony, but she needed to figure out a way to survive long enough for rescue to arrive. Despite the pain, Annette managed to drag herself to part of the smashed wing to collect the insulation. She used this to soak up the rain so that she at least had a viable, clean source of water. Standing to reach the insulation nearly drove her mad, and she was unable to place one foot in front of the other. To protect herself from the rain, she had taken a blue poncho she had found. However, this was the only thing she would take as her morals kept her from taking anything else. Even when her hunger became severe, she refused to touch the bodies around her.

Annette avoided looking at her fiancé, as she didn't want to break down from the emotional trauma. She would rather look at her ring and not at him. She refused to cry, believing it to be a waste of energy and crucial water. She survived on her instincts and heart while avoiding listening to her mind. She felt that her mind would make the situation worse than what she could handle. She spent a lot of time looking at the natural beauty around her.

She used yoga breathing techniques to help her cope with the collapsed lung, and it seemed to help. However, as each day passed, she was getting worse. Her hands were often covered in leeches, and her feet were severely swollen. Her toes were turning black, and gangrene was starting to set in her wounds. By Day 6, Annette felt that she was dying, as her kidneys started shutting down. She was surviving solely on the water she could collect when it rained.

Meanwhile, back home, her family had been notified of the

crash. Everyone believed her to be dead, and the newspaper printed a death notice about her and her fiancé. Her boss had even sent a condolence letter to her family. However, there was one person who refused to believe her dead. This was a colleague and friend named Jaime Lupa. He intended to fly to Vietnam with Annette's dental records and a brush containing her hair. Before he left, he promised to bring Annette back alive. This statement was not well received by her father, as he felt Jaime was a fool for holding out hope.

Day 7 after the crash, Annette went through a near-death experience, which was so moving, she was ready to die. She had made peace with what had happened. She became content to stare in amazement at the beauty surrounding her. On the day of her rescue, she was starting to slip in and out of lucidness, losing more of herself to delusion as the hours passed. Then, she heard a sound and looked in the direction it had come from. There was a man clad in an orange hoodie. This was a local policeman, later identified as "Mr. Cao". He left as quickly as he appeared, for this was the first time he had seen a Caucasian, and he mistook her for a ghost. He wasn't gone long, and soon, several Vietnamese workers came upon the site. However, this wasn't a rescue, but rather, a retrieval. They believed that no one had survived the flight and had only brought body bags with them. Stunned that she was still alive, they handed Annette a list of passengers and asked her to show them who she was. With few resources to carry the injured woman out of the jungle, the men had to fashion a makeshift stretcher using some canvas and two sticks. With the severity of Annette's injuries, the men even took off their shoes as they walked to prevent their footfalls from jarring her too much.

It was difficult for Annette to leave the crash site after being there for eight days. She had grown accustomed to it, and she didn't want to leave her fiancé behind to be claimed by the forest. She was sent to Singapore to treat her injuries.

On December 10, 1992, she attended William's funeral in Breda, Netherlands. She had to be carried in with a stretcher. She felt like she had been widowed by the plane crash, as she had spent a large portion of her life with him. By New Year's Eve, she was able to walk again, and by February 1993, she was back working at her old job.

KILLER TURBULENCE: WHAT CAUSED THE DROP IN FLIGHT VN474?

No true cause has ever been given as to why Flight VN474 crash-landed on that mountain on November 14, 1992. Yet, the most commonly-accepted theory is that poor weather played a role in it. Unbeknownst to Annette and William, Cyclone Forrest was developing in the Caroline Islands before their ill-fated flight. It wasn't until three days after its development that Cyclone Forrest was classified as a tropical storm in the South China Sea on November 12, 1992. Hints to how this storm affected the flight can be found in the weather information around Nha Trang. According to this data, there was some turbulence around the airspace and some cumulus clouds in the area. There were possible updrafts and downdrafts, both of which would have been associated with this type of cloud formation.

Annette mentioned air pockets being the reason why the plane dropped the first time and was likely right. An "air pocket" (otherwise known as "ordinary turbulence") is an area that has lower pressure in it than the surrounding area. This can cause planes to suddenly and unexpectedly dip.

Communication from Flight VN474 was lost two minutes before it was meant to land, and the wreckage was found about 12 miles (near Son Trung) from its intended destination. The likely reason the crash occurred close to the end of the flight was an accumulation of several factors. The first is that the pilot deviated

3.7 miles from the W-13 airway, likely to avoid the incoming storm front. However, this seemed to place the plane over a more mountainous area. Given that the aircraft dipped twice, according to Annette, it is likely the pilot wasn't at a high-enough altitude to clear the trees on the ridgeline. This is likely why Annette heard the motors accelerating, as the pilot may have been trying to correct the plane after the first dip. Unfortunately, it was the second dip that placed him below the necessary altitude needed to pass over the trees safely.

DEALING WITH THE LOSS AFTERWARD

Annette tried to cope with the loss of her life partner by jumping back into work, but she found she could never forget about him. Eventually, she was able to move forward. She married her colleague, Jaime Lupa, after some time. This had to be done in secret, as interoffice relationships were heavily frowned upon in finance at the time. Together, they had two children, a daughter, Joosje, and a son, Max. In 2001, nine years after the crash, Max was diagnosed with autism at the age of two. Because of this, Annette started working with parents of children who had autism. Sadly, the family broke apart in 2014 when Annette and Jaime divorced.

This wasn't the only tragedy that struck Annette after her rescue. In 2006, she returned to Vietnam, attempting to make peace with her past. Here, she learned that the men who had found her weren't the first to try and reach the crash site in 1992. There had been a Vietnamese Mil Mi-8 helicopter from Hanoi, carrying seven rescuers, one of whom was a doctor, which had tried to find the wreckage eight days after the crash. Sadly, the helicopter had gone down near Ô Kha mountain, killing everyone inside. She had had no idea until one of the family members had approached her and told her about the event.

Annette struggled with anger for a long time after the accident. She was angry about everything that had happened and how unfair life had been. It took some time, but eventually, she worked through her emotions about the crash. In 2014, she wrote about the ill-fated flight in her book, *Turbulence: A True Story of Survival.*

To this day, Annette still commemorates the crash on November 14. She thinks of how old William would be now while marveling at how she had managed to survive. She also takes the time to consider what she eats and drinks for eight days—from 7 a.m. on Day 1 to 8 p.m. on the eighth day. This is a representation of what she consumes now in comparison to what she had had available to her while lying on the jungle floor.

Despite Annette moving past the event which took away her fiancé, the families of the other victims couldn't. Many people were highly suspicious about the circumstances surrounding the crash. Some families got conflicting information about how the plane went down. One family was told that the plane had landed in the sea before being told that it had crashed close to Ho Chi Minh City with no survivors. Whether this was accidental or purposeful so as to not give the families any hope, we will never know.

Even the rescue was highly criticized. A Vietnamese doctor stated that more people would have been saved had rescuers tried to reach the wreckage on foot rather than going by air. It can only be assumed that the later aerial rescue by the helicopter was delayed because of Cyclone Forrest, which only dissipated around November 22, 1992.

As if that wasn't bad enough, some bodies were even sent to the wrong families. A total of three incorrect bodies were sent to grieving families. One family discovered this a day before burying the body sent to them, while another was forced to exhume the person they buried to make sure it was their family member.

4

CECELIA CICHAN: THE TODDLER WHO BECAME AMERICA'S ORPHAN

It's kind of hard not to think about it. When I look in the mirror, I have visual scars. –Cecelia Marie Cichan

One could only guess how excited and tired Cecelia was as she waited in the queue at Detroit Metropolitan Airport on the evening of August 16, 1987. She and her family were finally flying back from visiting relatives in Philadelphia. It was a lot of excitement for the 4-year-old. Her father, Michael, a botany professor, was likely thinking of the classes he'd have to give at Arizona State University. Her mother, Paula, who had just celebrated her 33rd birthday not too long ago, was likely trying to keep Cecelia and her 6-year-old son, David, from running around.

Soon, the family was seated on Northwest Airlines (now Delta Airlines) Flight 255. The McDonnell Douglas DC-9-82 (DC-9 Super 82) was filling up with many people flying back from Romulus, Michigan to Phoenix, Arizona. There were 149 passengers and six crew members that night. Perhaps there was some idle chatter before the plane fell silent, and everyone listened to the safety briefing. Cecelia likely didn't understand what was being said, as her seat belt was clicked into place for her. She was only too happy to hug her doll to her chest and admire the purple nail polish on her fingers.

One can only imagine the terror that was to follow when the plane took off at 8:46 p.m. EDT (0:46 UCT), only to result in a debris field spanning almost half a mile long a few minutes later. Flight 255 was about to become one of the deadliest air disasters in U.S. history.

THE DAY SHE FELL FROM THE SKY

Eyewitnesses on the ground and those in the control tower could only look on in horror as the plane banked soon after takeoff. It seemed to be rolling from side to side before the left wing struck a light pole in the parking lot of the airport's car rental building. This caused part of the left wing to be sheared off. Fuel stored in the wing was set ablaze, creating a cape of pure flame behind the plane. The right wing slammed through the roof of the car rental building, and now, there was no more controlling the aircraft's descent. The plane was upside down when it slammed into Middlebelt Road on Interstate 94 (I-94). It continued along the road, leaving debris and bodies for half a mile before it hit a railway overpass and burst into flames. Those on the scene not long after described the condition of the plane as "completely destroyed". Even those sent out to look for survivors doubted they would find anything. Yet, they still searched every body they found for signs of life, but with each deceased, the job was getting more and more difficult to do.

Soon, they realized that the dead were not just from the plane, but also from the road that was hit when it crash-landed. At that stage, a rookie firefighter, now a Lieutenant, John Thiede, was scouring through the debris, hoping against hope that he would find someone alive. As he moved, he heard a sound. It sounded like a toy doll crying. He looked around for the sound, as the passenger manifest had had several children aboard—some as unaccompanied minors. He soon found the source of the sound when he found a little arm poking out from under a chair. The fingers were decorated with purple nail polish.

Somehow, Cecelia had survived the impact that killed everyone on her flight (154 people) and two people in a car, while another five were injured on the road. Despite this, she was seriously injured. She had a fractured skull, a broken collarbone, had third-degree burns over 30% of her body, and her leg was broken. Initially, because of the confusion caused, it was believed that she was a victim from the road and not on the plane. Soon, this mystery was cleared up by Anthony Cichan, her paternal grandfather. He identified her by a chip in her front tooth and the purple nail polish the day after the crash. Sadly, many relatives of those on the flight—when learning there was a survivor—called the University of Michigan Medical Center to find out if it was their family member. Many of them had to receive the news that Cecelia wasn't their loved one.

Once Cecelia was conscious, she was able to tell nurses who she was, confirming Anthony's identification. Soon after, she was asking about her mother and demanded to have the doll she had had with her before the accident. She would remain in the hospital for almost two months, getting the necessary skin grafts and care required for her injuries. It was during this time that it had to be explained to her that there had been an accident and her mother, father, and brother had passed away. Mercifully, she had no memory of what had happened those few minutes before or during the fatal crash.

She was considered a "miracle child" for surviving a crash that saw the plane she was in destroyed. No one could understand how she had managed to survive. Some claimed she was found in her mother's arms, while others stated that her mother had shielded her from the crash. However, the bodies of her parents and brother were discovered away from where she was found still strapped into her seat. It is highly unlikely she was within her mother's arms at the time of the crash.

Despite her injuries, Cecelia made a full recovery. She became a well-loved and adored survivor, receiving thousands of gifts and cards from all over the world. She ended up getting so many gifts, her relatives asked to have them distributed to other children's hospitals. Later, a trust fund was set up by her family for her medical costs. Thanks to the generous donations from all over, it eventually totaled more than $150,000. Cecelia would be adopted by her maternal aunt, Rita Lumpkin, and her husband, Franklin. She would live with them in Birmingham, Alabama, shielded from those who wanted to get the story straight from a survivor's mouth.

ACCIDENTAL OVERSIGHT: WHAT CAUSED FLIGHT 255 TO BANK?

At first, no one was sure what had caused the horrendous crash. There were some speculations about a potential bomb on board or even the possibility of union sabotage. It took some time, but soon, the black box (a flight recorder, and usually a bright orange) was found. This box is a recording device that records conversations within the cockpit, as well as all other relevant flight data. It is heavily protected in the plane in case of an accident that could destroy the aircraft. Before this device is added to a plane, it needs to be tested to ensure its robustness. This includes underwater testing (up to 19,7000 feet), withstanding impacts (against a concrete wall while traveling over 460 mph), and even temperatures that can be as high as 2,000°F. Oftentimes, the black box is the only way to figure out what went wrong in a tragic event or even to find missing wreckages. Once the data was reviewed for

Flight 255, it was found that the crew had managed to skip some of the safety checks before takeoff.

According to the National Transportation Safety Board (NTSB), after their investigation, the crew had failed to check that the slats and flaps of the wings were properly set before takeoff. For an airplane to get enough lift during takeoff, because of the low speed it starts at, the wings need to have a greater surface area to create a larger airfoil. To get this greater surface area, the leading (front) and trailing (back) edges of the wing have moving parts called the 'slats' (front) and 'flaps' (back). When the slats and flaps are fully extended and pivoted downward, the camber of the airfoil is increased, therefore increasing the lift. When the flaps are extended by themselves, it helps to slow the plane down when it comes in for a landing.

Not having the flaps and slats in the correct positions before takeoff prevented Flight 255 from gaining the height and speed it needed to clear the necessary obstacles in its way. Although the finger was pointed firmly at pilot error, those of the crew weren't solely at fault. The captain, John R. Maus, was a 31-year-experienced pilot for the airline. He had thousands of hours under his belt. His copilot, David J. Dodds, was just as experienced, with over 8,000 hours in the air and over 1,000 hours on this particular model of plane. They were both competent pilots, so why did they fail to see that the flaps and slats weren't in the correct positions? Surely there must have been a fail-safe or some kind of warning?

The truth is that there *was* a warning system in place. However, for some reason still not explained today, there was an electrical fault that caused it to fail. This failure prevented the crew from realizing they were in danger as they continued to prepare for takeoff. It is likely that the crew knew as soon as the flight lifted into the air that something was wrong, but by then, it was too late for any corrective measures.

EMERGING FROM A LIFE OF OBSCURITY

The crash of Flight 255 brought out the best and worst that humanity had to offer. While people were scrambling to find survivors, there were several arrests made as people were caught looting the bodies and crash site. The tragic flight even took out a rising basketball star. Nick Vanos, an NBA center who played for Phoenix Sun, was tragically one of those who died on impact.

In 1994, a beautiful, black granite memorial was erected on the hill above the interstate where the crash took place. On the two outer panels are inscribed the names of those who tragically passed. On the central panel is a simple message from the Flight 255 Family, along with a dove holding a message saying, "Their spirit still lives on".

Relatives of those who passed ended up naming themselves the "Flight 255 Family", and every year, they would gather around the memorial to honor the day of the crash. They would share stories, a few laughs, and some tears as they spoke of those who had passed on. However, there was always someone missing. It was as if something was absent from the equation which could help them feel at peace with what had happened.

Cecelia's guardians had effectively hidden the girl from the world to protect her. They managed to achieve this, and she grew up living a normal life for the most part. She knew about the accident, and for a time, wasn't affected negatively by it. That was until late middle school or early high school. This was when the survivor's guilt set in, and she started asking herself questions as to why she was the one who survived and no one else. Many people tend to forget that even survivors are victims of circumstance. They survived, yes, but they may never see that as a good thing.

She was left with visible scars from the ordeal, which cover her forehead (that she hides with her hair), arms, and legs. Because of these scars, she thinks of the accident frequently. She considers these to be the scars forced upon her as she had no control when she was that age. That is why she got a tattoo of a plane on the inside of her left wrist. In a way, this was a scar she had power over, a way to control the situation she had been a part of against her will. She has no fear of flying, as she has no memory of the accident. Not only that, but she feels the chance of her being in another plane crash would be at astronomical odds.

Her life moved on, and in June of 2006, she married her high school sweetheart, John Benjamin Crocker. Lieutenant John Thiede walked her down the aisle and shared a dance with her. She was now happily married and studying art therapy, and she felt that her life was complete. Even then, she still didn't talk about the accident. That was until she was approached to help with the documentary, *Sole Survivor,* in 2011.

On May 15, 2013, a special screening of *Sole Survivor,* held in Royal Oaks, Michigan (close to where the plane had crashed), was shown to the relatives of those who had died in Flight 255. They were shocked and amazed when they got to hear from Cecelia. It was the first time in 26 years that they had seen or heard anything about her. To many, she was the missing connection to their loved ones, someone who had been absent from their lives for so long. To many, it felt like the wound of losing their family members was starting to heal. She helped many families recover from this trauma. Cecelia took a tragic event and managed to build a life for herself and heal those around her.

5

MARIA NELLY MURILLO: HOW A MOTHER'S LOVE CONQUERED ALL

I thank my God for allowing me to save these two people. –Acisclo Rentería, Red Cross volunteer.

Saturday, June 20, 2015, Captain Carlos Mario Ceballos was going through all his safety checks before getting his twin-engined Cessna T303 Crusader (designated HK-4677G) ready for the flight he had planned. He was traveling from Nuqui Airport in Columbia to Quibdó. It was a short trip, only 30 minutes, as both locations were in Chocó. It was a flight he had done many times before. Sometimes he would fly cargo, but other times, his plane would be used to charter people back and forth. Despite the closeness of Nuqui to Quibdó, the route through the jungle was dense and difficult to navigate.

He looked over to his passengers. He knew taking this trip on foot would have been particularly difficult for them as the 18-year-old Maria would have had to carry her infant son with her. The boy, Yudier Moreno, was less than a year old. Captain Carlos likely hoped that the baby wouldn't make too much noise as they flew.

The remaining cargo on his plane was about 500 pounds of fish and some coconuts.

Once he was sure everything was in order, with permission from the control tower, he got the trip underway. For 20 minutes, the plane was visible on the radar, but then it suddenly vanished. Those at the airport tried to reach the pilot, but when they couldn't raise him on the radio, they knew something terrible had happened. They immediately sent out a rescue plane while contacting the authorities. Soon, the police, fire service, and the Red Cross had joined the effort to find the three individuals who had gone missing in the Columbian jungle.

This was not a safe area to go down in. It is known for poisonous snakes, illegal gold mines, contained drug smuggling routes, and there was a chance the survivors may come across armed groups of people who were battling for control over the different coca plantations in the area. 'Coca' is a plant that contains the psychoactive alkaloid known as 'cocaine'. As if those weren't the only dangers to possible survivors, this area was also known as one of the wettest places on Earth. With near-constant rain, the exposure would kill anyone quickly if they weren't able to find shelter. The rescuers were on a tight schedule to locate the survivors.

THE DAY SHE FELL FROM THE SKY

The crash into the Serranía del Baudó mountain range (Northwestern Columbia) had instantly killed Captain Carlos. The cockpit had been all but destroyed. However, possibly due to the fish taking the brunt of the impact, Maria and Yudier had survived the crash. The collision had caused a fire to start in the cockpit and was spreading fast. Maria, understandably terrified, pushed the cabin door open and tried to flee. In the nick of time, she remembered her son and dove back in to retrieve the child. He escaped with nothing more than a few charred pieces of clothing. However, his mother wasn't as lucky. She had a fractured ankle, some first and second-degree burns on one arm and leg, and a gash on her foot. Considering what she had been through, she had come away lucky.

Fearing that the plane may explode, Maria rushed away from it uphill. Concerned for her child, she looked him over and found he was warmer than normal. She stopped to bathe him in a pool of clear water. Once his temperature was stable, she tentatively returned to the plane to see what she could scavenge. It was here that she came across a machete, some coconuts, cellphones (hers and the pilot's), and everything she had carried with her.

Thinking that she could call for help, she tried the two phones. Unfortunately, one was dead, while the other had no credit to make a phone call. Despite this, she tried to make over 90 calls, but due to the poor signal, she wasn't able to reach any emergency services. Fearing that she may have to spend the night in the jungle alone with her infant son, Maria started heading toward a small river she had spotted. She was hoping to find help from anyone she met along the way.

She was concerned, though. She knew that someone would come looking for the plane, and she didn't want to be too far from it when help arrived. As she moved through the jungle, she left a small trail of items to show people where she had gone. She found a small ravine a little later and managed to set up a roof that offered some shelter from the rain. She didn't have much food, but she did have coconuts and a way to open them.

Then Maria remembered the fish on the plane. Unfortunately, she didn't remember how to get back to the plane—despite having tried to lay a trail—and fearing she'd get lost in the jungle, decided to stay put until help came to her. This started her five-day ordeal in the jungles of Columbia, surviving on nothing more than coconut water and water she gathered when it rained. Although she tried to trap rodents as another form of food, she was sadly unable to do so.

Rescuers scoured the route between Nuqui and Quibdó, both by air as well as on foot, in hopes of finding some clue as to what had happened to the Cessna T303. It took them two days (now Monday) before someone in the air noticed a white spot in the jungle. Once on the ground, they found the body of Captain Carlos and what remained of his plane. The first thing rescuers noticed was that the cabin seemed almost untouched by the crash landing. They also noted that the cabin door was slightly ajar. At first, they weren't sure if this was because of the accident or because survivors had managed to walk away from the crash.

They opted to have faith in the latter as they checked the passenger list. They soon realized that they were looking for a young woman and an infant. They searched the area and didn't find any bodies or blood. This convinced them that the mother and infant somehow survived the initial impact, but may now be lost in the jungle or worse.

The 14 rescuers on the ground refused to give up and started searching for signs of Maria's passing. Soon, they managed to find some. They located some cracked coconuts, the useless cell phones, a discarded flip-flop, and the baby's birth certificate, which had been placed by a tree. This wasn't just haphazard debris from the crash; this had been purposefully laid out as a trail. The rescuers just had to follow it to find Maria.

Despite this, it took another two days (now Wednesday) of searching before the rescuers became desperate in their search. A Black Hawk helicopter was brought in to help with the search. It was specially fitted with loudspeakers which continued to play the same message over and over again: "Nelly, please come back, we're looking for you", or, "Nelly, we want to hear from you". The helicopter continued to circle overhead, hoping to lure the woman out from where she was, but after some time, this didn't happen.

Now exhausted, rescuers were getting ready to call off the search for mother and child. They started debating between each other if they had the strength for a few more minutes of searching or not. The group agreed and continued to trek through the jungle. Acisclo Rentería, a 38-year-old Red Cross volunteer, and three rescuers found their way to a ravine about 0.3 miles from the crash site. The first thing Acisclo noticed was a swarm of flies. Thinking the worst, he and the other rescuers rushed forward to find Maria and her son lying on the ground.

Hearing people calling to her, Maria tried to struggle to her feet, calling out for help over and over. Her injuries were starting to get the better of her, and she couldn't walk towards the rescuers. She was half-starved, exhausted, and in shock, but alive, and so was her baby. Although he was a little cold and had an irritated bottom, the baby had made it with his mother.

Maria asked for food and water as soon as she realized she had been saved. For the next four hours, the rescuers fed her crackers and water slowly, allowing her strength to build. Acisclo held the baby close to keep him warm while he cleaned his mouth of debris. Maria was so grateful for the rescue and food, she asked Acisclo to be the child's godfather.

The rescuer felt that this was a blessing to him, despite being unemployed and being displaced from his hometown due to the conflicts in Columbia. He joined mother and son as they were airlifted from the area. He continued to hold onto Yudier as they were flown to Quibdó for treatment. Everyone was surprised that the infant had managed to stay alive through the ordeal. The only reason he had managed to not only survive, but also remain uninjured, was his mother's drive to keep them both alive. As she had access to coconuts and water, she was still breastfeeding her child and keeping him fed during those five days.

Once the pair were initially checked at a hospital in Quibdó, they were soon sent to a better-equipped hospital in Medellín.

Here, they would spend some time recovering from their ordeal. By thinking of shelter, water, and food, Maria was able to not only keep herself alive, but also her infant son, who would not have made it on his own. She is a true testament to all parents who would do anything to give their children a fighting chance at life.

JUDGMENT LAPSE: WHAT CAUSED HK-4677G TO FLY INTO THE GROUND?

When looking at the wreckage of HK-4677G, it is difficult to understand how the cockpit was practically destroyed while the cabin was barely damaged in comparison. However, when reading over the investigation, it starts to make sense. According to the investigation done by Aerocival, the crash likely occurred because of a poor risk assessment by the pilot.

It is believed that the flight was made using visual flight rules (VFR) conditions to go over the mountainous area. The VFR are regulations that the pilot operates the aircraft in conditions that are clear enough for them to physically see where they are going. It is likely the conditions at the time of flight were not suitable for the pilot to follow VFR. Because of this choice, rather than choosing instrument flight rules (IFR) when the weather turned poor, the pilot was unable to see what he was doing. Weather, such as blinding rain, haze, or even flying through thick cloud cover, is known as "instrument meteorological conditions" (IMC). When these conditions occur, the pilot needs to rely on their instruments over their physical vision.

Sadly, it is likely that HK-4677G was at too low of an altitude when trying to clear the mountain, as the pilot had lost his situational awareness in regards to his plane in relation to the ground. He unintentionally flew his plane into the mountain because he couldn't see where he was going.

LIFE OF ANONYMITY

Sadly, after the initial reports of the miraculous survival of Maria and her baby, nothing more was ever reported on the pair. This is likely due to the two of them living in the underdeveloped part of Columbia and not generating enough attention in the rest of the world with their story. Despite surviving a plane crash, they were—and still are—practically unknown.

If Maria and Yudier are still alive as of 2022, then it can only be hoped that their lives, which had been spared that fateful day on June 20, 2015, are being lived to the fullest. Maria would likely be around 25. Maybe she has had more children and spends her day keeping them out of trouble. Yudier may be almost 8 years old and likely completed his first year of school. Perhaps he has developed a talent for playing sports, writing, or even singing. Though his mother will vividly remember surviving the crash, he will mercifully not remember anything. It can only be hoped that the two of them are living their best possible lives right now.

6

MIRACLE IN THE JUNGLE: JULIANNE KOEPCKE'S ORDEAL IN THE AMAZON RAINFOREST

I learned a lot about life in the rainforest, that it wasn't dangerous. It's not the green hell that the world always thinks. –Juliane Koepcke

Juliane Margaret Koepke was born on October 10, 1954, in Lima, Peru, to doting parents Maria and Hans-Wilhelm Koepcke. Both her parents were from Germany and had moved to Lima to pursue their work. Hans-Wilhelm was a well-known biologist, while Maria was a well-known ornithologist.

Juliane was a bright student, who hoped to one day follow in the footsteps of her parents, and soon that dream was to become a reality. Between December 22 and 23, 1971, she attended her high school dance and graduation in Lima. Maria had wanted to leave Lima a few days (December 20) earlier to meet her husband in Pucallpa, but Juliane really wanted to attend these two events. Her mother relented and booked them a flight to take them to Pucallpa on December 24, even though Hans-Wilhelm was against them using LANSA. However, this was the only airline which still had a flight left, and Maria was sure everything would be fine.

Juliane's joy and excitement of getting to see her father was overshadowed on the day when the plane was seven hours late to the Jorge Chavez International Airport. The flight was LANSA Flight 508, and the plane on the runway was a Lockheed L-188A Electra turboprop with the registration OB-R-941. The flight, containing 86 passengers and six crew members, would take about an hour.

Once she was seated in seat 19F, Juliane's excitement returned to her. Everything seemed fine, and the other passengers were just as cheerful, filled with the Christmas spirit as they stowed away their luggage and gifts. The takeoff was uneventful, and the passengers even got to enjoy a sandwich 30 minutes into the flight. This calm would change when the plane flew into what appeared to be a thunderstorm. Maria was starting to get a little nervous, but Juliane was fine. She, after all, loved flying and wasn't worried. She trusted the pilot's skills. Soon, the plane was swallowed by the darkness. For the next 10 minutes, the turbulence got worse and worse. Items from the luggage hold were strewn across the plane, and the passengers were notably getting more upset as the plane was rocked by the turbulence.

Lightning forked across the sky, and now Juliane was starting to echo her mother's concern. The two women gripped hands, too terrified to speak, and continued to look out of the window Juliane sat next to. Despite the storm's ferocity, the pilot didn't turn the plane around. It would forever doom Flight 508, as just about 15 minutes from their destination, lightning hit the outer engine where Juliane was sitting.

Now deadly calm, Maria said, "That is the end, it's all over."

Juliane would only realize much later that these were the last words she would ever hear her mother say to her. The plane lurched downward before it went into a nosedive. Nothing the crew did could bring the plane back under control, and the wings couldn't handle the strain. Juliane's ears were filled with the sounds of the engine and people screaming before it went eerily silent. Somehow, she was now freefalling outside of the plane, and the only sound she could hear now was the whistling of the air as she plummeted to the ground.

She was still strapped into her seat. Next to her, the seats that had been occupied by her mother and an unknown gentleman, were now vacant. She didn't have time to think or even feel as she was fast approaching the Amazon Rainforest canopy headfirst. A combination of g-force and pressure mercifully allowed her to pass out before she slammed into the thick canopy of trees.

THE DAY SHE FELL FROM THE SKY

On Christmas Day, Juliane awoke, bruised and battered, but miraculously alive. Somehow, the nearly 100-foot thick canopy had not only cushioned her fall, but also managed to upright the seats so that she didn't land on her head. Despite this, she did have a concussion and was deeply in shock. What she didn't know was that she had just survived falling 10,000 feet from a plane that had broken apart in midair.

Despite being awake, she was dizzy and unable to get to her feet, losing consciousness several times that day. It wasn't until Boxing Day that she was finally able to get to her feet and started looking for any other survivors in the general area. She cried out in Spanish, German, and English, hoping to catch anyone's attention. She was desperate to find her mother. Sadly, there was nothing in the area except for a bag of candies, which she would continue to eat for the next four days. She hadn't walked away from her sudden descent injury-free. She had broken one collarbone, had several lacerations to her legs, a bad gash on her upper right arm, a swollen right eye (which she struggled to see through), and a ruptured ligament (ACL) in her knee.

Despite these injuries, she found she could move around with very little pain—likely from the shock. She knew she couldn't stay there. She could hear the planes overhead, searching for the crash site. Unfortunately, they or Juliane couldn't see each other through the canopy. Juliane needed to find a way to get someone to help her and staying where she had landed wasn't a good option. She became frustrated with her situation, which melted away into despair. She needed to get moving before she lost herself to her emotions.

The Amazonian jungle is thought of by many as a dangerous place, as it contains poisonous animals, snakes, and jaguars. You'd think that this would be of some concern to the injured girl. However, for a year and a half, she had spent time with her parents at Panguana research station—founded by them in 1968—not 30 miles from where she was now, though she didn't know this at the time. During her time at the research center, Juliane's parents had taught her about the jungle and how to survive in it. She had no fear of what the jungle held.

However, she was poorly dressed to survive the elements. At this time of year, the rainforest was experiencing its rainy season, and it would rain several times during the day and night. While the daytime temperatures would reach as high as 104°F, the nighttime temperatures would plummet to 68°F. All Juliane was wearing was a sleeveless mini dress and a single white sandal. The other one had been lost during her fall. That wasn't the only thing that had been lost. Suffering short-sightedness without her glasses, Juliane found navigating through the forest a difficult task, one she had managed to tackle with what she had available to her.

As she walked, she would test the path before her by throwing her remaining sandal ahead. She had hoped this was enough to frighten off possibly-camouflaged snakes, ones that hide among the leaf litter of the forest floor. Even with this technique, she still feared possible animal attacks. Her second fear was starving to death, especially after the sweets ran out.

Eventually, she found a small creek, and the training her father had given her kicked in. A creek inevitably leads to a stream, which will join a river. If she continued to follow it downstream, there was a chance she could come into contact with other humans. The plus side of finding the creek was that she could walk in it without fearing where she placed her feet.

By Day 4, after the crash, Juliane's attention was caught by a strange sound that struck fear in her heart. It was the sound of a king vulture landing, and she knew this sound quite well. She also knew this sound meant that the bird had found some carrion to feed on. As she rounded a bend in the stream she had been walking in, she came face-to-face with a sight that horrified her enough to be paralyzed.

There was a bench from the plane, but unlike her bench, this one had been driven three feet into the ground, headfirst. It contained the bodies of three passengers: two males and one female. If the fall hadn't killed them, the impact did. This was the first time Juliane had ever seen a dead human body. At that moment, she believed her mother was one of those bodies, despite knowing that her mother had been next to her on the flight. She needed to be sure. She took a stick to knock off the shoe of the woman in the seat. Once off, she could see that the woman had painted her toes, something Maria never did. Juliane was immediately filled with relief, but soon, that feeling was replaced by shame for how she felt. She had to move on.

By Day 10, she was too exhausted and weak to continue walking. She opted to float down a river, occasionally swimming a little instead of plodding along the banks. Although there are piranhas in the Amazon jungle, she knew they tend not to go after larger prey unless they are injured or already dead. A school would have had to be at least 400 members strong to strip a human to the bone. After some time in the river, she realized she had received severe sunburn to the back of her shoulders. It was so severe that it was later considered second-degree burns.

During this time, Juliane was falling into despair from loneliness and was starting to give up hope. Although she had had plenty of water to drink, she hadn't eaten for the last six days and barely had any strength. This is likely why, when she saw the boat, she first thought it was a hallucination. She had to go right up to the boat to touch it before realizing it was real. Close to the boat, she found a path that led up a slope. She was so weak, she had to practically crawl up it to reach the top. There, she found a native-style hut that had a palm-leaf roof. Inside, she found the onboard motor for the boat and a barrel of gasoline.

The sight of the gasoline reminded her of something her father had had to do to treat an injury the family dog had received, which later became fly-struck. This would end up helping Juliane, as she had a problem with flies as well. In the forest, the insect life was relentless, and as her injuries became infected, flies became attracted to them. This resulted in the wound in her upper arm becoming infested with maggots. She struggled a little to open the barrel, but as soon as she could, she found some tubing and siphoned some of the gasoline to treat the injury in hopes of killing the maggots. At first, they tried to bury deeper into her arm, bringing her a lot of pain before they started to die. She was able to remove about 30 of them, and she was quite proud at remembering the trick her father had used.

It was starting to get late, and she had been looking for a place to rest that night. So, Juliane spent the evening in the hut. The next day—Day 11 after the crash—it continued to pour with rain, and she decided to remain in the shelter. She had thought of taking the boat to get help, but she was so weak, she just couldn't bring herself to do it. Toward late afternoon, she was sure that she had heard voices. To her, it sounded like angels. It was some local lumberjacks who eventually stumbled upon her, and they were shocked. At first, they believed that they had found the water spirit, Yemanja, a local legend many of them believed in.

Thankfully, Juliane didn't have to suffer a language barrier after all she had been through. She was able to communicate with the men about who she was and where she had come from. Realizing the gravity of the situation, they took care of her wounds and gave her some food. The following morning, they all traveled together to the closest lumber station. It was from here that a willing pilot took her to the closest hospital to be fully treated for her injuries.

Her father, hearing about her miraculous survival, traveled to meet her. He had been so sure he had lost both his wife and daughter. There were barely any words exchanged between the two of them before they embraced each other. Hans-Wilhelm was convinced that since his daughter wasn't seriously injured, surely his wife would have made it through the crash as well.

Thanks to the directions Juliane gave after being questioned by the air force and police, they soon found the crash site. It wasn't long before they were able to locate the bodies of those who were on the plane. On January 12, 1972, Hans-Wilhelm was asked to view the bodies that had been found. Sadly, his wife Maria was among the dead. Tragically, she had survived the initial impact, but had later succumbed to her wounds. She hadn't been the only one. Besides Juliane, 14 others had survived the fall, only to die hours or even days later.

It would take a long time for Juliane to trust planes and pilots after what she had gone through. Eventually, she managed to fly again, but she was constantly nervous, and every little, strange sound made her think the plane was going down once more. She was thrust into the spotlight; it was a fame she never wanted, and it prevented her from mourning for some time. She even suffered from recurring nightmares for years after the event.

GROSS NEGLIGENCE: THE REASON FLIGHT 508 WAS TORN APART

What most people take from the story of Juliane is that the pilot had made a mistake flying into the storm. What they don't realize is that there were several terrifying incidents of gross negligence on the part of Líneas Aéreas Nacionales Sociedad Anonima (LANSA). For the most part, if there is a crash, it is commonly determined that the pilot is at fault. When looking at the number of responsibilities a pilot has, it only takes one slip up to result in an accident. However, this isn't the only reason a fatal plane crash can occur.

Mistakes by crew members, such as not securing baggage or failing to do their duties while on board, could result in injuries or possible deaths. Although they may not contribute to a fatal crash, any death in the cabin is still an unnecessary death and shouldn't happen on a plane if it can be helped. Then there is the maintenance, or rather, lack thereof. Many companies like to use the term "money-saving measures", and unfortunately, sometimes this can result in disaster. Cutting corners with maintenance or outsourcing it to places not licensed to do so puts the plane and its occupants at risk. This outsourcing can even result in poor standards of inspection.

The design and manufacture of parts of an aircraft need to be of the best quality. Parts or designs which have defects can lead to the integrity of the plane failing when it is needed most. They need to be strong enough to handle all stresses placed on the plane while it is operational.

Sometimes, even weather can be blamed for a crash. However, with enough warning, these can be avoided or dealt with adequately. Occasionally, it may even be best to ground the plane until further notice, which leads to the next problem: the negligence of airline corporations. Time is money, and the more time wasted, the less money they are making. This results in the cutting of corners to allow for quicker turnabout times. This can cause inadequately-filed paperwork, exhausted crews, and a poorly-prepared aircraft, all of which is a ticking time bomb.

Even an air traffic controller who is inattentive for a moment can send the wrong plane to the wrong runway. These people are meant to be the eyes and ears of the planes. By not paying attention to what they are doing, they put the lives of many people in multiple planes at risk.

In the case of Flight 508, the blame was placed squarely on the shoulders of LANSA. On that fateful day, all other outbound flights had been grounded because of the storm. This wasn't true for Flight 508; it was the only one still willing to fly. Why? Because the crew was under pressure to meet all the demands of the holiday schedule. This was why, when the pilot realized that the storm was worse than he imagined, he couldn't risk flying back.

At this stage, LANSA already had a poor track record of reliability, as seen with the plane being seven hours late. The Lockheed L-188A Electra was one of the last planes LANSA was using, and it was basically cobbled together from spare parts of other planes. This brings us to the mechanics who worked on the plane. The work on the plane was done by those who didn't have the correct training to work on the vehicles. They were more familiar with cars and motorcycles. This led investigators to believe that the plane was poorly serviced and maintained. Even the pilot didn't have his paperwork in order, as his license had expired long before the flight. Whether this was an accidental oversight or no one bothered to check is up to anyone's guess.

It is believed that when the lightning hit the engine, as described by Juliane, it caused a fire. This caused the engine to malfunction, causing the plane to enter its nosedive. Despite the crew trying to straighten the plane, the force on the wings (especially the one with the damaged engine) was too much, and they tore away from the fuselage. This caused the plane to break apart in midair, resulting in many passengers being thrown from the plane to freefall. Those not buckled in would freefall without any wreckage to help slow their descent or cushion their fall.

LANSA was forced to suspend all their flights. Later in 1972, after being stripped of their airline license, they closed their doors forever.

LIVING LIFE TO THE FULLEST

By March 1972, Juliane was well physically recovered from her ordeal. She wanted to return to Lima to continue her studies. Her intent was to study in Lima for two years before completing the entrance exams in Germany. However, the media hounded her to get her miraculous survival story. This ended up causing her father to have a nervous breakdown. He sent her to live with her aunt and grandmother in Germany, banning her from returning to the Panguana research center. This caused a rift between father and daughter, but Juliane complied with Hans-Wilhelm's wishes, despite her desire to return to Panguana. A few years after this, her father would return to Germany as well.

Juliane's survival piqued the interest of millions of people around the world. Her story resulted in a fictionalized movie, *I miracoli accadono ancora* (*Miracles Still Happen*), in July of 1974, before being translated into English in 1975. It was directed by Giuseppe Maria Scotese and starred Susan Penhaligon, who played Juliane. It wouldn't be the last time Juliane's story would be told. In 1979, Jim Anderson published *Crash in the Jungle*, describing what Juliane went through.

Juliane graduated from the University of Kiel in 1980 with a degree in zoology, but she wasn't done with her studies. She was considering getting her doctorate but wasn't sure what she wanted to base her study on. Her father suggested she study the bats around Panguana. Surprised by her father's suggestion, Juliane didn't hesitate to return to Peru to get to work on her studies. Within 18 months, she had identified 52 different bats in the area. She published her thesis in 1987.

Then in 1989, she married Erich Diller—an expert in parasitic wasps—and changed her surname. They still continue to fly to the research center twice a year together. In 1998, Juliane was approached by Werner Herzog, a director, to film a documentary about what she had been through. Werner had a specific reason for this. He had been filming *Aguirre, the Wrath of God* during the later part of 1971. If it hadn't been for a change in his schedule during December, he would have been on Flight 508. At first, Juliane didn't want to be a part of the documentary, but eventually, she relented.

Together, they flew to visit the crash site, which still remains in pieces in the Amazon jungle. Coincidentally, the seat she sat in was 19F, the same seat she had occupied on Flight 508. The experience was therapeutic and allowed Juliane the closure she needed about the crash. Werner released his documentary, *Wings of Hope*, on February 01, 2000, in Germany. While they were working together, Werner convinced her to preserve her parents' legacy and the work they had done on Panguana. She continued to work with the Peruvian government to expand the research center. This resulted in the initial 460 acres her family had started with to grow to 1,730 acres. This is an area of the Amazon jungle that doesn't allow human colonization, logging, or hunting. To this day, Juliane is still dedicated to protecting the rainforest.

The work on the documentary caused Juliane to start the research on writing her own memoir, *Als ich vom Himmel fiel* (*When I fell From the Sky*). While researching for the book, she came across letters her father had written, and a few things started making sense. She came to believe that the reason her father had forbidden her from returning to Panguana was that she looked so much like her mother. It would have been his first year without his wife and seeing his daughter around the research center while he dealt with his grief was just too much for him to handle. Sadly, her father had died in 2000, and she couldn't confront him about her find. Following his death, she became the director of Panguana and was in charge of organizing the research expeditions to the center.

Her memoir was originally published on March 11, 2011 (under her maiden name), while the English translation was published on November 01, 2011. The book was so moving, it received a Corine Literature Prize in 2011. In 2016, a children's book titled *Juliane fällt vom Himmel* (*Juliane falls out of the sky*) was released, allowing younger audiences to learn about what Juliane had gone through.

As of 2022, Juliane is still working at the Bavarian State Collection of Zoology, located in Munich, where she and her husband still live. She advocates for people to always live their life to the fullest. Rather good advice, as you may never know when your last day could be.

7

NESTOR MATA: THE MAN WHO SLEPT THROUGH A PLANE CRASH

I was given a precious life when I survived the fatal crash of Douglas C-47 plane Mount Pinatubo on Mount Manunggal in Balamba, Cebu, 55 years ago. –Nestor Mata

President Ramon del Fierro Magsaysay Sr. arrived in Cebu City on March 16, 1957. He had a very busy day around the city, and it was almost at an end when he had dinner with the mayor of Cebu City, Sergio Veloso Osmeña Jr. After that, he went straight to Lahug airport to travel home. With him were a few high-ranking Philippine government ministers, some civilian and military aids, and three journalists, one of whom was Nestor Mata.

Nestor was born in 1926 and started his career in journalism in 1947 at the age of 21. In 1949, he started reporting for the *Philippine Herald*. He even became their war correspondent in 1953. Later that same year, he was assigned by his newspaper to cover the newly-elected president. Now at 31 (four years later), he was reporting on the much-loved eighth president of the Philippines as he carried out his duties. He was due to fly back with the president, but Mayor Sergio wanted him to remain the rest of the night in the city. It was close to midnight, and though Nestor was tempted, the president wanted to get home soon. Nestor made the decision to fly back with the president.

When they arrived at Lahug airport, the presidential plane was ready to take them home. The twin-engine Douglas C-47A-75 DL was named "Mount Pinatubo", after a then-inactive volcano in Magsaysay's home province of Zambales. This was a refurbished plane with under 100 hours of flight. It was operated by the Philippine Air Force and was flown by Major Florencia Pobre, a trusted pilot.

Tonight, there would be five crew members and 21 passengers. Being quite tired, Nestor boarded, took up his seat, and almost immediately fell asleep. He was only two seats away from the president's compartment, close to the cockpit. He felt safe and comfortable enough to sleep on this trip, as he trusted the pilot not only with his own life, but also with the president's.

While Nestor slept, Major Florencia went through all the safety checks and prepared the plane. They were flying to Nichols Fields, 400 miles away, close to Manila. The weather was perfect for flying. It was described as fine, with a bright moon and some clouds. By 1 a.m. on March 17, 1957, the plane took off, though it seemed to be struggling. According to some eyewitnesses, the plane didn't appear to be gaining the altitude it would need to crest the Balamban mountain ranges. It was this flight that resulted in the vice president, Carlos Polestico Garcia, becoming the next Philippino president just one day later.

THE DAY HE FELL FROM THE SKY

Soon after takeoff, the final communication received by Mount Pinatubo was to those of the Malacañang Palace (the presidential home) to pick up the president at 3:15 a.m. from the Nichols

Fields. Nothing indicated that anything was wrong with the plane at this stage.

Yet as the time passed, the appointed pick-up time came and went with no plane in sight, and those at Nichols Field started becoming concerned. The president's family would only be told later that morning that the flight had gone missing, and no one knew where it was.

The Philippine Armed Forces scrambled and led the search for the missing plane over land and sea. They were assisted by the United States Navy and Air Force. They mostly concentrated on searching the ocean for any signs of wreckage, as the majority of the flight was over open water. At first, the news was slow to spread, but within a few hours, it made its way to the masses. Hundreds of people were noted to openly weep at the loss of the flight, and potentially, their president.

Nestor's sleep had been disturbed by a bright, white light, but instead of waking fully from his rest, he lapsed into unconsciousness. Eventually, he awoke to stare at the bright moon above him. Momentarily confused as to where he was, he checked his Longines watch and found it to be 3 a.m. Coming to his senses, he found that he was on a steep cliff. He was lying on some leaves, but was surrounded by bushes. What he had thought to be a nightmare at first was starting to reveal itself as the truth. This was when he realized that something terrible had happened.

Although he was in agony, he sat up and looked around him. The wreckage of Pinatubo was about 10 feet away from him, still on fire. Horrified, Nestor's eye fell upon several benches torn from the plane, which contained unmoving forms of people he had spoken to only a few hours prior. Despite him calling out to the president and Pablo Bautista (a reporter for *Liwayway Magazine*), there was no answer. He soon realized that he was the only person to survive whatever had happened. He also remembered that he had never put his seat belt on before falling asleep. It was likely that he had been thrown from the plane during its impact with Mount Manunggal in Balamban, Cebu.

The pain he was feeling was from burn injuries he had sustained to his arms, legs, and part of his abdomen. Realizing he was in danger, Nestor started shouting for help, hoping someone would hear him. He was in luck, because something *did* hear him. A dog named 'Serging'—named after the mayor of Cebu—had heard him and howled in reply.

Knowing that a dog meant some form of civilization, Nestor kept calling for help. His voice carried through the mountains, and by 8 a.m., he was discovered by some farmers from the area. Unfortunately, they had nothing to carry him down the mountain, so they had to return to their village. Luckily, they soon came back with a hammock made of bamboo.

Marcelino Nuya—the village captain—led 11 other rescuers to carry Nestor from the mountain. The climb down was treacherous, and one misstep would have sent all 13 men down the slope, killing everyone. Yet somehow, they managed to not only make it down the slope unharmed, but continued to walk 18 hours to carry Nestor to civilization. Most of this time was done in the blazing sun, which caused Nestor's raw burns to develop blisters.

He was taken to the Southern Island Hospital in Cebu City. There, he was treated by Dr. Jose V. Agustines. He was suffering from shock, as well as second and third-degree burns over his body. While in the hospital, despite the pain, Nestor didn't lose consciousness. He dictated what had happened to a nurse who sat by his bedside while being treated. This press dispatch stating that President Magsaysay was dead was sent to his newspaper, which got the story about the president's death with all the facts from the only survivor. Nestor was a journalist even while he was suffering. He would later be transferred to Veterans Memorial Health Center in Quezon City.

Nestor roughly guessed that the accident occurred at 1:40 a.m.

He felt that he had survived because God had a higher purpose for him, but he had to figure out what that was. We are left to wonder why he survived. Why had he survived an impact with a mountain when he hadn't worn a seat belt? There are a few possible theories that can explain this. By not wearing a seat belt, he didn't suffer the same crushing forces as those who had their seat belts on. Then you have to consider what he was doing when the impact occurred. He was asleep, completely relaxed.

When looking at motor vehicle collisions, there are cases of drunk people surviving horrific accidents with barely any wounds. Why? Generally, their motor functions are impaired, making them slow to react to the accident. This includes them tensing up at the point of impact. Sober drivers tend to tense up at this point as well. This can either be by extending their arms or trying to reach for something during the crash. By going rigid, these drivers' muscles constrict, which results in more injuries when there is a sudden deceleration of the vehicle. This also reminds us that the correct brace position can protect against more severe impact injuries.

It is possible, that by being more relaxed, Nestor's body was able to absorb more energy—and lower the force on his body—at the time of impact. This would explain why he had no typical impact injuries, such as broken bones, and only suffered from burns. It may have also helped that his fall was cushioned by the vegetation around the crash site.

Military rescuers arrived at the crash site—about 22 miles away from Cebu City—on March 18, to locate and identify the bodies of those from the flight. The president was identified by his brother by the watch that he wore. This was later confirmed by his dental records. The Philippines went into mourning, and roughly five million people attended his burial on March 31, 1957.

ONE-IN-A-MILLION FAILURE: WHY THE PINATUBO HIT A MOUNTAIN

Before any investigation had started, it was thought that the plane had been sabotaged. President Ramon was a *Nacionalist* (Nationalist) and very popular. It was believed that he would be reelected during the voting in November 1957. However, before he had become president, he had been elected as the Secretary of Defense on August 31, 1950. During that time, he had led a fight against an insurgency of the communist-inspired Hukbalahap (Huk) movement. It was theorized that the plane was possibly sabotaged as an act of revenge. However, as time progressed, no evidence was found to support this theory. There were other theories, ranging from a drunk or sleepy pilot, to the plane being overloaded, to it exploding in midair. None of these were ever proven.

Eventually, the cause of the crash was determined on April 27, 1957. While testifying to the Senate committee, General Manual F. Cabal stated that the cause of the accident was metal fatigue on a spindle driveshaft. This was considered a preliminary finding and was never presented to the Flight Safety Foundation.

It was believed that soon after takeoff, the spindle driveshaft in the right engine carburetor snapped. Spindle shafts are responsible for creating a mixture of fuel and air during a flight. By creating different mixtures, the plane would have the power to fly at different elevations. Once this spindle broke, the right engine didn't get the correct mixture of fuel and air, resulting in a loss of power.

Although this was officially accepted by the Senate, these driveshafts rarely break. This, coupled with the plane having flown less than 100 hours and being refurbished, made it difficult to believe that a faulty part was missed during the inspection. Despite this, the broken spindle driveshaft is widely accepted because of the presidential plane's crash. Coupled with the eyewitness testimony of the plane struggling to gain enough altitude, this cause was determined to explain the plane's condition the last time it was seen. As one engine was getting the correct fuel and air mixture, the plane could still climb, but not enough to get over the mountain range.

COLORFUL LIFE AFTERWARD

Despite what he had to endure, being carried down from the crash site, Nestor went on to live his life to the fullest that he could. He would spend months recovering from his injuries. He continued to write for newspapers and magazines, wrote books, played chess, learned to appreciate art, and even taught himself to sing classical music. This meant he had to learn to sing in German, French, and Italian. He dedicated his life to what he described as "telling the truth and shaming the devil".

He felt that the crash had managed to shake his shyness and doubts from his body. He started by writing his take on the plane crash. *One Came Back* was cowritten with Vincente Villafranca and published in 1957. Nestor even liked to joke about how the burns never damaged anything below the belt. He went on to have two more children after the accident, ending with a total of five.

He spent over 60 years as a journalist. Even after he retired, he continued to write and taught countless generations of writers. He continued to write for the *Philippine Herald* till the paper was closed by Ferdinand Marcos, who had declared martial law, in 1972. Not allowing this to get in the way of his passion, Nestor moved over to *The Daily Express*. Here, he would work till 1986—when Ferdinand was ousted—writing columns about foreign affairs instead of politics. Then he made the jump to the *Manila Standard* to write about art and political columns. Not only was he a columnist from 1986 to 1999, but he was also the coexecutive editor for *Lifestyle Asia*. He continued to write columns for the *Malaya* newspaper (originally called *Ang Pahayagang Malaya*) from 1999 until his death. This is just his impressive list of work achievements. He also taught political science at the University of Santo Tomas until 1972.

Having had a childhood filled with music and the love for it, Nestor finally gained the courage to express himself with it. Every year, he would give a classical concert to a private audience made up of friends and fellow musicians. He considered *Dein Ist Mein Herz* by Franz Schubert to be his favorite song. He felt that music renewed and energized him, so he continued with his yearly tradition. He even played chess and won a few events.

Having lived a full life, which was nearly cut short when he was 31, Nestor sadly died on April 12, 2018, at the ripe old age of 92. The man who had had a booming voice, with a unique laugh, was considered gruff, yet friendly, and had lived a marvelous, colorful life. He will never be forgotten by those whose lives he had touched with his teaching, writing, and survival story.

8

ESCAPE FROM A DEADLY INFERNO: JAMES 'JIM' POLEHINKE'S STORY

Why did God do this to me? –James Polehinke

Comair Flight 5191 was due to leave Blue Grass Airport in Lexington, Kentucky before dawn on August 27, 2006. The 47 passengers were bound to Hartsfield-Jackson Atlanta International Airport in Georgia. The early Sunday flight would be done in the dark, with some rain inbound from the west. There were three crew members on this flight. Captain Jeffrey Clay and First Officer James Polehinke were in charge of getting everyone to their destination.

As they prepared the plane before getting it ready to taxi onto the runway, they chatted a little. Jeffrey was talking about his two young children, while James spoke about his four dogs. The atmosphere between the two was pleasant despite the hour of the flight. As they continued their preparations, the passengers were being shown to their seats and listening to the safety briefing. Nothing seemed amiss, and two previous flights had already left from Runway 22 earlier that morning.

Runway 22 was approximately 7,000 feet long, just enough to

get the Bombardier CRJ-100 airborne and on its way to Georgia. Flight 5191 was cleared for the takeoff of this runway. Still chatting while the plane was taxiing into position, Jeffrey was in control until it came time to take off. At this moment, James commented that it was weird that the lights on this runway weren't on. It wasn't yet morning, but none of the lights were activated. Jeffrey just responded with an affirmative that it was indeed weird. Neither of them felt it pertinent to let the flight control tower know what they were seeing. They assumed that they were in the right place, and if they weren't, the tower would have confirmed and corrected their course.

Now in position on the runway, James was given the controls. In the dark and with approaching rain, the copilot started the aircraft down the runway. The last word he heard from Jeffrey was 'woah', as the plane traveled off the end of the runway much sooner than expected. It was barely getting airborne before its landing gear caught on a perimeter fence, causing the plane to go down in a nearby field. It hit a few trees before it broke apart and burst into flames. Flight 5191 had crashed before it had had a chance to take off.

THE DAY HE FELL FROM THE SKY

What had just happened was that James had tried to take off from Runway 26 and *not* Runway 22. This runway was half the length of Runway 22, not nearly enough distance to allow for a safe takeoff for the plane James was flying. The lights on this runway hadn't worked correctly since October 2001. It was only meant to be used during the day and by much smaller planes.

Once the plane had overshot the runway, it was too late to do anything. It didn't have the necessary speed or power to go over the fence and trees on the other side of Runway 26. As the plane had just been filled with jet fuel, the intense fire caused by the crash would soon build to inferno levels. For the most part, the plane was intact, so there was hope that someone had survived the crash.

First responders were on the scene almost as soon as the crash had occurred. They knew they needed to work fast if they were going to save anyone. Police officer Bryan Jared was one of the first people on the scene. He was the one who noticed James moving around in the cockpit and dove in to save the first officer despite burning fuel hitting him. He was able to pull James from the wreck with only some minor burns to his elbow. Sadly, the inferno grew in intensity, and soon, the rescuers were unable to get to anyone else who may still have been trapped in the wreckage. They were forced to watch as firefighters tried to extinguish the blaze, with no luck. All involved were deeply shocked at what they had witnessed.

While rescuers were desperately trying to get to those left in the wreck, James was rushed to the University of Kentucky hospital. He was severely injured, and at first, it wasn't believed that he would survive. A team of doctors and nurses worked round the clock to save his life. By the time they were done, James was on a ventilator and in a coma, but alive. His injuries were numerous. The impact had caused multiple facial fractures, three broken ribs, a broken sternum, a severely broken left leg and ankle, and a broken hand. He also had a complex pelvic fracture, a collapsed lung, two spinal fractures, and there was a likelihood that he would suffer from brain damage if he ever woke from the coma.

While James lay in a coma, the investigation for the crash was carried out by the National Transportation Safety Board (NTSB), while autopsies were performed on the bodies, which were eventually recovered. Of the 50 people on Flight 5191, James was the sole survivor of the impact and fire. Once the autopsies were concluded, it was found that 16 passengers had suffered from smoke inhalation. This meant that they had survived the impact, but had perished due to smoke inhalation and the high temperatures of the burning jet fuel.

The families of those who had died in the crash wanted answers as to why the plane had been on the wrong runway. Likely pressured to give an answer, it was announced that the incident likely occurred due to a pilot error. Generally, in fatal plane accidents, the pilot and copilot are typically the first to die. This is because the nose of the plane usually takes the brunt of the impact, causing the cockpit to be destroyed, instantly killing those in it. Yet, in this instance, the nose hadn't impacted the ground, and the copilot had managed to survive. He was the one who held all the answers now. However, he was also the one who could be blamed for what had happened. It was likely that there already were people who laid the blame for the crash at James's feet.

It took some time for James to recover from the accident. He remained on the ventilator for some time before being taken off it. Though most of his injuries healed over time, the damage to his left leg, spine, and brain were irreversible. Despite several operations, his left leg never recovered and needed to be amputated. He was left paralyzed from the hips down, and the brain damage caused him to forget everything from before the flight and during the crash. He wouldn't be able to give any meaningful information to investigators.

While recovering from his injuries, he didn't speak much about the crash, so his doctors encouraged his family not to hound him for answers. For a long time, he was barely able to move anything more than his head, and often, he had tears in his eyes. Whether it was from pain or realizing what had happened is anyone's guess. He spent many days fading in and out of consciousness. It was clear, early on in his recovery, that he was suffering from severe survivor's guilt. He wanted to know why God had done this to him. His mother, Honey Jackson, would tell him that the crash had not been God's intent, and that it was all just an accident.

Surviving the ordeal had been a living hell for James. His wife, Ida, commented that it is likely that he would have preferred to have symbolically gone down with the plane, as Jeffrey had. James would remain in the hospital for a lengthy stay before going into rehabilitation.

THE PERFECT STORM: WHY FLIGHT 5191 FAILED TO TAKEOFF ON THE CORRECT RUNWAY

When an investigation reveals that there was a pilot error, the first thing people demand to know is if the pilot was qualified to fly in the first place. James had been flying since 1997 when he joined Gulfstream International Airlines (which no longer exists due to bankruptcy) in Florida. He flew with them until 2002 and was experienced in flying twin-engined planes for short ranges. He was promoted to captain in 2000 while flying with the airline. Information about pilots with bad reputations will make the rounds quickly among other pilots, but this wasn't the case with James. His previous colleagues had nothing but praise for the pilot while he worked for Gulfstream. He had an excellent reputation with a clean record of no accidents or mistakes. He then started working for Comair in 2002. Even the President of Comair, Don Bornhorst, stated that the crew was experienced and had flown the plane used in Flight 5191 multiple times.

The NTSB even went so far as to test the pilots' blood to see if either of them were under the influence of alcohol or other illicit substances. The only thing found was a decongestant in James's blood, which was an over-the-counter medication not on the banned list.

Despite the preliminary findings of pilot error, the NTSB did a thorough investigation of the crash and everything that led up to it. The usual suspects included engine problems, which were quickly eliminated. They then started to question why Jeffrey had taxied the plane onto Runway 26, as it had been planned that Flight 5191 would takeoff on Runway 22. They had no clearance to be on Runway 26 at all. Both the pilots knew that Runway 26 was too small for their commercial aircraft; they should never have been on it. Why were they, though?

Runway 22 and 26 both shared the same taxiway—a route that joins to a runway—which had been altered due to construction a week before. The construction was a repaving project which had caused changes in the taxiway usually used between Runway 26 and 22. At the time of the investigation, it wasn't established whether either of the pilots had flown from Blue Grass since these changes were made. The Federal Aviation Administration (FAA) had notified airlines who flew into Blue Grass Airport about the changes to their airport surfaces. However, it was noted that the maps and charts used by several airline pilots, including the ill-fated Flight 5191, hadn't been updated to reflect these changes. It was likely that the two pilots mistook Runway 26 for Runway 22.

Even when James queried that the runway had no lights, neither of the pilots confirmed with the traffic control tower whether they were on the correct runway. It would also seem that neither of them checked their navigational instruments before takeoff commenced. If they had, they would have realized that they had been on Runway 26, which faced more westerly in comparison to Runway 22, which ran more southerly. This would have caused them to get a confirmation from the tower as to their location on the airport surface.

Generally, a plane stops before takeoff, doing final checks and communicating with the tower. In the case of Flight 5191, the plane only paused for about 45 seconds before it made a rolling takeoff, as it was cleared to do so. Although rolling takeoffs are not against any aviation rules—and are considered normal—it is generally only done on busy runways when there is a lot of traffic on the same runway. This quick decision to get the plane into the air may have contributed to continuing on the wrong runway.

On January 17, 2007, the NTSB officially released their findings on the investigation. It was their belief that the crash was likely caused due to pilot error. The investigation felt that both pilots failed to use the available cues and aids to help them identify the plane's location to the airport's surface. This led to them choosing the incorrect runway for takeoff. By not checking their navigational instruments to ensure that they were on the correct runway, they had removed the only safeguard that had been in place. However, other experts felt that this was an easy answer to a more complex problem, and that several other parties were at fault in parallel to the pilots. The investigation had highlighted multiple other issues surrounding the crash, leading many to believe that this was more of a systems accident than solely a pilot error.

Flight 5191 wasn't an isolated incident. According to NASA's Aviation Safety Reporting System (ASRS) report 256788 (37000 Feet, n.d-a), during November of 1993, a medium-sized commercial jet was cleared for takeoff on Runway 22. Before commencing takeoff, the pilots decided to check their departure routes because there were storms in the area, and it was already raining at Blue Grass Airport. They quickly realized their heading was incorrect to what it should have been if they were on Runway 22. The traffic control tower contacted the pilots to cancel their takeoff, as they were on Runway 26. Eventually, this flight would successfully take off a little later on the correct runway.

Those involved in the incident felt that there had been several contributing factors as to why the pilots ended up on the incorrect runway. The first was that there was poor visibility with the weather. Secondly, the runway intersections were confusing. Lastly, the tower called for an immediate takeoff, which likely could have added to the pressure of needing to take off without double-checking everything. Luckily, these pilots did take the time to check their instruments before commencing takeoff. After this incident, it was suggested that a warning be made to help clarify which runway is which for any that have multiple ends.

Despite this, even after Flight 5191, there was another incident during the same month that NTSB released their findings on Flight 5191. This time, it was a Learjet (LJ45), and according to NASA's ASRS report 722668 (37000 Feet, n.d.-b), the plane turned onto Runway 26 when it was meant to be on Runway 22. Luckily, the mistake was spotted, and the plane eventually took off from Runway 22, successfully.

Yet it wasn't just the confusing taxiway that caused Flight 5191 to crash. It was a series of smaller incidents that created the perfect storm. It started with the idle chitchat between Jeffrey and James. In 1981, the FAA brought about the sterile cockpit rule. This meant that during taxiing, takeoff, and landing, there should be no irrelevant chatter in the cockpit. Although most of their conversation occurred before taxiing the plane into position, some of the irrelevant chatter spilled over while the plane was taxiing toward the runways. This was against the federal regulation. Usually, it isn't odd for pilots to speak about irrelevant topics while taxiing, but Jeffrey and James pushed their conversation to a limit, which was considered a rare event. It was likely that this idle chatter caused the pilots to become distracted and not see the changes to the taxiway. This contributed to their loss of positional awareness.

The maps and charts used in the cockpit weren't updated. They may have been unaware of the changes made to the surface of the airport. As both pilots have flown from Blue Grass Airport before, they both should have been aware that Runway 26 was unlit. When James noted that there were no lights on the runway, either he or Jeffrey should have queried it with the tower to confirm where they were. Questioning this seemingly irrelevant event would have immediately alerted the tower to the incorrect position of the plane. It is likely the two pilots didn't cross-check the plane's position, as they believed that they were on the correct runway. They were influenced by confirmation bias.

It was also discovered that the pilots never received the paperwork from Comair that detailed the changes to the taxiway. The whole week leading up to the accident, the controller had made announcements about the changes, but it hadn't been announced that morning.

Another fatal error was that there was only a single person in the traffic control tower that worked overnight. According to FAA regulations, there should have been two officers: one to deal with the radar and another who was meant to keep an eye on the grounds. Christopher Damron, the lone controller on duty, told the pilots that they were cleared for takeoff on Runway 22. He concentrated on the radar more than watching what the plane was doing. Once the plane started taxiing, he turned away from observing it, assuming that there wouldn't be a problem. He then turned his back on the plane to complete administrative duties instead of monitoring the aircraft to ensure that it was on the correct runway. He continued with this task until he was interrupted by the crash and subsequent fireball to the west of the airport.

The overnight traffic control tower had already been understaffed as of May 2006, when a controller retired. The tower manager during this time, Duff Ortman, only had high praise for Christopher despite what had happened. He even cited that the young man had prevented two planes from getting into a loss of separation situation. This usually occurs when two planes come too close to each other in the control zone. He had caught this because he was working together with another controller. He was also well-liked by everyone he worked with, earning their respect. The investigation also had concerns about the fatigue and training of the air traffic controllers, as they were so understaffed.

At the beginning of the investigation, the mistake made by Christopher was listed as a contributing factor that led to the crash. However, the blame was shifted to the pilots by the end of the investigation. It was also found that the FAA was partially to blame, as they had failed to enforce recommendations made earlier for there to be runway checks. Sadly, this tragedy was based on a series of human errors. This was a case where there wasn't a single fault that could be blamed, but rather, several, making pinning the blame on one thing very difficult.

LESSONS LEARNED FROM TRAGEDY

As with many other crashes, after an investigation is completed, regulations and safety procedures get updated. Sadly, it takes a tragedy for certain procedures and regulations to be accepted and implemented. Some of the changes seen after Flight 5191 were significant. The first was that pilots should move away from maps and charts in favor of installing an automated moving-map system into the plane. This would allow pilots to check whether they are on the correct runway or not. However, this isn't feasible for all airlines and may take several years to see the changeover.

Commercial flights were no longer allowed to take off from unlit runways, and there was a call to improve the lighting. In 2010, the FAA made it a requirement that all pilots get clearance from air traffic controllers at every runway crossing. Regional airports were encouraged to improve their signs on the airport surface to make them more visible. There was even a movement to address the fatigue experienced by those in control towers overnight.

Despite all these changes, the families of those who perished in the crash found the facts revealed by the NTSB hard to endure. Just *how* had so many things gone wrong? Most focused on the fact that the pilots were at fault, and since one was still alive, he was worthy of their hate and animosity.

Despite surviving, Jim never fully recovered from the incident.

After spending weeks in the hospital, he was released in October of 2006. From here, he spent a further two and a half months at Cardinal Hill Rehabilitation Hospital, learning to cope with his drastic lifestyle change. Despite this, he still has to use a wheelchair to get around.

To this day, Jim still suffers from severe survivor's guilt and blames himself for what happened. This causes him to descend into what he describes as "dark places", ones he struggles to come out of. At his side is his wife. She is his caregiver and has been supportive through all of this, allowing him to grieve appropriately. He still has good days and bad days and just takes them as they come. Because of his paralysis, the couple moved away from Florida and took up residence in Colorado. Here, Jim had more opportunities to take part in adaptive sports.

The only reason he was able to survive the crash was due to the prompt arrival of first responders. Had he not been removed from the cockpit when he was, he would have likely died like the rest onboard.

Five years to the day after the crash, a memorial was erected in honor of those who had passed. The 17-foot tall memorial—a circular piece of granite as a base, with the names of the victims and 49 silver birds in flight toward Heaven—can be found in the rose garden at the University of Kentucky Arboretum. Understandably, Jim was not at the unveiling. During this time, he had managed to live a life away from the spotlight and scrutiny of the public. That was until Ky Dickens approached him, just as she had approached Cecelia and Bahia. She wanted to give him the platform he needed to speak and deal with the trauma he had gone through.

On July 18, 2013, there was a private screening of *Sole Survivor* at the Kentucky Theater, Lexington, for the families of those lost in Flight 5191. There was a noticeable increase in tension when Jim's story was presented. There was still a lot of animosity over what had happened, even after seven years. People still stayed and listened because it was the first time Jim spoke about the incident for an extended period.

By the end of the screening, there was a mixture of new emotions. There was still some hate for what had happened, but there was also now an understanding that the one left behind had suffered... and was still suffering. People were starting to understand what he had lived through, and they pitied him. Despite surviving, he had lost a lot and still struggles physically and emotionally with what happened. Jim was, and still is, as much a victim as what the deceased are.

9

HOPE AMONG THE DESERT DEBRIS: THE STORY OF RUBEN VAN ASSOUW'S MIRACULOUS SURVIVAL

I don't know how I got here, I don't know anything else. I just want to get going. I want to get washed, dressed, and then go. –Ruben van Assouw

Patrick and Trudy van Assouw had a treat planned for their sons Enzo (11) and Ruben (9). The couple was celebrating their copper wedding anniversary—traditionally done at 12 and a half years in the Netherlands—and wanted to go somewhere special. Once spring vacation was upon them, the whole van Assouw family would be traveling to South Africa to have the safari trip of a lifetime. The boys were so excited that they could barely sleep before the trip. Patrick was also excited, so much so that he had started a travel blog on April 26, 2010. He used this platform to tell his family and followers what they were up to.

They spent two days flying from Brussels to South Africa. The flight hadn't agreed with young Ruben, who was motion sick and vomiting by the end of the trip. They were picked up by a man—at 5 a.m. at O.R. Tambo International Airport in Johannesburg—carrying a sign which misspelled their family name to "van Besouw". Patrick laughs at himself for confusing the windscreen wipers for the indicator a few times while he gets used to driving on the opposite side of the road. By 2 p.m. that afternoon, they were officially in their camp, starting to relax for their holiday. The car trip had also caused poor Ruben to get sick.

From April 28 to May 9, the family would travel through South Africa, stopping at several tourist destinations. This included Pilgrim's Rest, God's Window, the Kruger National Park, Swaziland, St. Lucia, and Lesotho (now known as 'Eswatini'). During their time traveling, they got to experience all the natural beauty the country had to offer, as well as a host of animals that are only seen in Africa. This included the Big Five (elephant, rhinoceros, African buffalo, leopard, and lion), for which the Kruger National Park is well known. Enzo was the first to spot elephants and was quite proud of himself.

Despite all the travel and going to different camping sites, the children made a few friends in St. Lucia when playing on the beach. They even exchanged their email address with their new friends before they left.

One of the last entries in the travel blog explains the sheer number of stamps which went into the family's passports as they crisscrossed the northeastern parts of South Africa. The final entry to the blog described everything the family was doing on May 9.

On May 11, the family was preparing to leave South Africa and travel back to the Netherlands. They were flying on Afriqiyah Airlines Airbus A330–202, registered as 5A-ONG. Flight 771 (sometimes referred to as 8U 771) would be a seven-hour-long trip to Tripoli, Libya. There would be 93 passengers and 11 crew members on this flight.

Despite Patrick's blog, the whole family was eager to tell their friends and family about what they had seen and experienced. Their bags were stuffed with trinkets, most of which were carved, wooden animals that they had picked up during their travels. They couldn't wait to get home in the next few days. Ruben, at this stage, was probably hoping he wouldn't be sick on their plane again. He was eager to tell his friends how he had herded sheep away from the first camp they had set up.

The plane took off at 19:25 UTC, already pretty late for the young boys, who would likely sleep all the way to Libya with some luck. The family likely dreamed of returning home that night. Patrick was probably thinking about his final update to their family vacation for his blog. Sadly, the blog would never be updated. As of 2022, the blog still contains the comments and messages left by those mourning and those wishing Ruben a speedy recovery.

THE DAY HE FELL FROM THE SKY

The flight had been completely uneventful during the night. There had been no reported technical issues by the pilot, copilot, or relief copilot. The flight was standard... until it wasn't. As the plane was coming in for landing at Tripoli International Airport, there was a call for a go-round, which the control tower accepted. The plane started its miss approach procedure. The aircraft seemed to increase in altitude before it suddenly descended, slamming into the sandy lot in front of the runway it was destined to land on. This occurred just after 6 a.m. local time (4 a.m. UTC).

This impact caused a trench almost 500 feet long and 80 feet wide. The speed at which the plane had collided with the ground was so high that the aircraft practically disintegrated, throwing debris everywhere as it traveled further due to inertia.

On the ground, the tops of several trees were sheared off, a car was crushed (mercifully, no one was in it at the time), and the debris struck the side of a house at the end of the lot. Luckily, the house remained mostly intact, and those who were sleeping inside were not injured. They were awoken by the impact and rushed outside to see what had happened. There wasn't much to see, but they were overwhelmed by the smell of jet fuel, and soon, the air was filled with the sound of ambulances and fire trucks.

Rescuers swarmed the area in hopes of finding any survivors. This included a security agent–described as elderly–who took one look at the bodies and debris strewn everywhere and collapsed. He had been suffering from diabetes, and the shock caused an increase in blood sugar, which reached dangerous levels. He dropped dead on the spot. Flight 771 had just claimed a soul, and he wasn't the only one.

Very little of the plane remained fully intact, with the exception of the tail section. The debris field was several hundred feet long with plane debris, luggage, and bodies. The rescuers were forced to check each person they found to see if there was any life. The longer they looked, the more hope they lost.

At the end of the debris field, about half a mile from where the tail was found, rescuers came across a seat which contained a child still strapped into it. Not holding out much hope for a young child to have survived the accident, the rescuers tentatively moved forward with their duty. With shock and euphoria, it was discovered that the young child was still breathing. They jumped into action.

The boy was Ruben, semi-conscious and unresponsive due to shock. He was bleeding moderately from leg injuries, but overall, seemed unhurt. Once the rescuers started moving him, the shock wore off, and he became more lucid. The pain in his legs was now starting to affect him. However, rescuers noted that though he was in pain, he didn't cry too much.

Ruben was rushed to Al-Khadra Hospital, where he was treated for several fractures between his two legs. The surgery took about four and a half hours to complete. His only other injuries included blood loss and a bruised and swollen face. Somehow, the boy had managed to avoid all the other usual impact injuries seen in plane crash victims. Surgeons were amazed that he had no internal organ damage or severe injuries to his head and neck. It was hard to believe that he, alone, had managed to survive after Flight 771 was torn apart. One reporter from *The Associated Press* had stated that the boy's survival was because God had wanted it so.

Although heavily medicated, when Ruben was conscious, he was well-aware of his surroundings and interacted with all who spoke to him. Unfortunately, he had no memory of the plane's impact on the ground. This is similar with many survivors of crashes—either from shock or when suffering a concussion.

Within a day of hearing about the accident, his paternal aunt, Ingrid van Assouw, and his uncle, Jeroen van Sande, were at Ruben's bedside, comforting him. They were forced to tell him about the death of his brother and parents later in the week. Flight 771 had lost 103 people.

Three days after the accident, Ruben was to return to the Netherlands. He was bundled up on a stretcher with a blue blanket and a cap and scarf to protect his face as Libyan reporters swarmed him for a photo opportunity. Those carrying him were forced to cover the boy's face so that he could have some privacy. He traveled from Matiga Military Airfield with his uncle, aunt, and Dr. Siddiq ben Dilla, the Libyan doctor who had been treating him. He would remain with the boy and continue to treat him until he was no longer needed.

Ruben's uncle and aunt asked that the press give the family some time before asking any questions. They were currently dealing with two hardships: the loss of family and a child who was injured and likely traumatized. Once home, he would be hospitalized in St. Elizabeth's Hospital in Tilburg, until he was well enough to be released.

Back in Tilburg, Netherlands, where Ruben had been living with his family, a bouquet of white flowers was propped against the front door. In the Netherlands, white is considered the color of mourning, and that is what the country was doing as they had lost many of their citizens.

FAILED COORDINATION: WHAT BROUGHT FLIGHT 771 DOWN?

Everyone was left with the question of what had happened. The flight had been normal before the plane hit the ground in front of the runway. There was talk of this crash being a potential terrorist event, but as time progressed, this was proven to be false. There was so much debris spread over such a large area, that it would be difficult to get a better picture until the black boxes were recovered.

Tripoli International Airport may not have had the latest in known aviation equipment, but they had been operating safely for years before this event. Even the plane that had crashed had just had its safety inspection and had a clean safety record. It was serviced on March 15, 2010. Overall, the Airbus 330-202 was known to have a safe reputation. How did Flight 771 crash on its final approach to Runway 9? To find out the possible answers, the Libyan Civil Aviation Authority (LCAA) worked together with France's Bureau of Enquiry and Analysis (BEA), the Netherlands' Dutch Safety Board (DSB), South Africa's Accident and Incident Investigation Department (AIID), and America's NTSB and FAA. To aid these departments of investigation, Airbus and General Electric also sent people to help find out what went wrong.

The captain of the flight had been a captain since 1988—he had been working for Afriqiyah since 2007—and had amassed over 17,000 hours of flying time throughout his career. He had over 500 hours on the particular plane that had crashed. His proficiency wasn't in question, as it had been checked on November 15, 2009. He was even considered one of the best pilots Afriqiyah had to offer. His two copilots had also passed their proficiency checks and had similar time spent flying on the Airbus 330-202. Neither had the same overall experience as the captain. All of the pilots' blood was tested, and their systems were clear of any alcohol or drugs. They also had over 15 hours rest at O.R. Tambo International Airport before flying to Libya. This didn't rule out the possibility of fatigue, as this was an overnight flight.

The plane had come down 4,000 feet before Runway 9. It had left a debris trail of over 2,600 feet when it collided with the ground, traveling at 260 knots (300 mph). It was established Ruben likely survived because he had been assigned a seat closer to the front of the plane (seat 12D). Although this was the seat assigned to him according to his ticket, it is unknown if the seat he sat in *was* seat 12D. He could have changed his seating position with anyone in his family. All other victims had died from massive trauma.

With concerns over the condition of the plane and pilots being addressed, the investigators turned to other potential contributing factors. The weather at the time of the crash was indicated as hazy, with one flight landing before Flight 771 having indicated that they had gone through some low-level stratus clouds and experienced patches of fog. However, these sorts of weather conditions are normal around sunrise, which occurred at 4:11 a.m. local time on the day of the crash. These conditions are known to crews who fly into the area.

Next, they turned to the information from the black boxes to determine what had occurred in the cockpit. This was when the mystery started to unravel. Flight 771 had commenced a go-round on their approach to the airport. This is when a landing is aborted either on the final approach or after a quick touchdown. This is done when a pilot feels that the conditions on the runway are not safe, and it is safer to get the plane back into the air or keep it in the air. Reasons for go-rounds are done when not able to land in the touchdown area (too high of an altitude), speed is too high (can cause the plane to overshoot the runway), another plane is on the runway which hasn't taxied away yet, or weather conditions, such as low cloud or fog that obscures the runway, are present.

When a go-round is decided, a pilot determines what their next course of action will be. They can try to circle around before attempting to land again. Alternatively, if the conditions are too unsafe, the plane will divert to the closest airport. This is a standard event that may be shocking to the passengers, but generally, it is well thought out and planned by the person landing the plane.

Sadly, this isn't what had occurred with Flight 771. First of all, the information about the weather conditions to the crew didn't properly reflect the conditions at the time of the accident. These weather conditions would deteriorate until Runway 9 was closed about an hour after the accident. The weather was so poor, that when the plane passed the TW locator, it was already flying 200 feet under the recommended altitude of 1,000 feet. They were trying to spot the runway through the haze. The approach continued to be lower than the minimum descent altitude (MDC), and the captain had informed the air traffic controller that he would report once he spotted the runway. At 280 feet, the Terrain Avoidance and Warning System (TAWS) started giving a warning of low terrain. With the runway not in sight, they needed to do a go-round.

However, the copilot, who was the pilot flying (PF), hesitated. Then the captain, who was the pilot not flying (PNF), told him to go round. They were now dangerously low to the ground. The crew couldn't get any visual references, and this led to what is known as "somatogravic illusion". This occurs when the acceleration of the plane is confused with an increase of pitch altitude (the nose of the plane is higher than the tail).

At this stage, the copilot and captain didn't share a common action plan as to what to do with the final approach to Runway 9. The captain took the controls and had started inputting instructions into the instruments, but he failed to announce that he had control. During the last few moments of Flight 771, both the captain and copilot had control over the plane. This went against the standard operating procedure implemented by Afriqiyah. With limited cooperation and coordination between the two men, likely suffering from the somatogravic illusion, there were more nose-down inputs applied to the instruments while the plane was in its go-round phase. This is why, at first, it seemed like the plane was gaining altitude before it suddenly descended and hit the ground.

In the end, it was determined that the crew resource management (CRM) had deteriorated between the two pilots, causing too many incorrect instructions to be given to the plane. There had been too many nose-down commands, which were not consistent with what should have been done during the final phase of flight. The CRM is vital to the crew, as it is in place to reduce errors, determine leadership, help with decision-making, and even aid in interpersonal communication. Once this broke down, there was no communication, which caused zero coordination between the two pilots. Simply put, one didn't know what the other was doing, and this led to the plane crash-landing before it was close to the runway.

The investigation concluded that the cause of the accident was brought on by the deterioration of the CRM between the cockpit crew. They also felt that the weather played a role, and that Runway 9 should never have been used under the conditions it was experiencing. They also cited the lack of training by the crew in cases of nonprecision approaches. This is when an approach is done with instruments, utilizing lateral guidance by itself with no vertical guidance. Fatigue may also have played a role in how the pilots handled the situation in the cockpit.

ADAPTING TO LIFE AFTERWARD

As with the case of most young children who suffer from traumatic events, their families try to shield them as much as possible. This is crucial to their healing process, as they often need to be protected from members of the media who don't always practice the necessary tact. Upon returning to the Netherlands, Ruben was taken in by his extended family before he was eventually adopted by his uncle and aunt. He was raised alongside his cousins without the constant interference of people wanting to know his story. After all, he had no memory of the accident. His family effectively managed to hide him away from a prying world. As of 2022, Ruben is likely in his early twenties.

Although his actual story ends here, it doesn't end completely. On January 6, 2020, Ann Napolitano published her book, *Dear Edward*. She had been deeply moved by the event, which resulted in Ruben losing his family, and yearned to know more about the person who had survived. Unfortunately, she couldn't find any information about him, thanks to his uncle and aunt shielding him so effectively. She decided to write a fictional book loosely based on the events of Flight 771, about a 12-year-old boy who was the sole survivor of his own horrific plane crash.

Wherever Ruben and his remaining family are today, it is with great hope that he found peace with what happened and got to live the life his parents had envisioned for him.

10

GEORGE LAMSON JR.: THE MAN BEHIND BRINGING SOLE SURVIVORS TOGETHER

I don't want to be remembered as the boy who survived this accident. I want to be remembered as the man that lived. –George Lamson Jr.

On January 20, 1985, it was Super Bowl 19, and the two teams clashing were the San Francisco 49ers and the Miami Dolphins. The San Francisco 49ers managed to take the victory by 38 to 19, but George Lamson Jr. didn't care. This trip with his father had been an amazing bonding experience, and he wouldn't have traded it for the world. Besides the Super Bowl, he had some time to go skiing that afternoon. He was just an ordinary 17-year-old teenager. He had the same concerns and chores as any other kid his age. Yet all of that melted away that weekend with his dad, George Sr.

All good things had to come to an end, though, and by the end of the day, both father and son went to Reno-Cannon International Airport (now known as Reno-Tahoe International Airport) to get home. They would be flying back from Reno, Nevada to Minneapolis, Minnesota. It was already late, almost the next day, and both men were tired from all the excitement of their trip. They were flying in a chartered Lockheed Electra L-188, four-engine turboprop (N5532), and they weren't the only ones. Galaxy Airways Flight 203 was full of fans who had enjoyed Super Bowl weekend in Reno, but now, they were eager to get home. There were 65 passengers and six crew members. The flight would take several hours, and George Jr. was already exhausted.

Once he and his father boarded, they got seated, and George Jr. was settling down for a nap. This would be disturbed when two men approached the pair and declared that the seats they were sitting in were theirs. This couldn't be the case, as there was no seating chart, and anyone could sit where they wanted. It was first come, first served. Despite this, George Sr. was in no mood to fight, so he and his son moved and found themselves some new seats. They ended up sitting in 6A and 6B, junior and senior, respectively. Now sitting closer to the front of the plane, they were directly behind a bulkhead.

Once everyone was seated, the cabin crew prepared for takeoff and gave the safety briefing. It was likely during this time that George Jr. ensured his seat belt was tightly fastened. Flying was meant to be safe, but you could never be too careful. After 1 a.m., the flight took off. A little over a minute later, George Jr. would still be strapped in his seat, as he was thrown forward 40 feet to skid to a halt on South Virginia Street.

THE DAY HE FELL FROM THE SKY

The takeoff went smoothly for a while, but then the plane was hit by what felt like turbulence. It felt as bad as when George Jr. had flown through a storm during a previous flight. He also heard two thumps that seemed to be coming from the right side of the plane. Then, the aircraft started to turn toward the right. George Jr. could see stars through the window on his left. The plane was losing altitude fast, and before he knew it, he heard an announcement being made on the public address system that they were going down. A crash was imminent. Despite the shock, George Jr. knew he needed to brace for the impact, or he would be seriously injured. Just before the impact, he managed to cover his face with his arms and pull his legs up to his chest.

The plane hit the ground and bounced. It would bounce three times before it hit an RV sales lot and broke apart. It had been traveling at 140 mph. Somehow, during the impacts, the bulkhead in front of George Jr. tore open, and he was flung through what he described as a 'fireball'. Still strapped into his seat, he skidded some distance before landing on the highway nearby.

Soon after the crash, the traffic control tower contacted the rescue workers, who rushed to the scene. There had been some confusion at first, as some people believed an 18-wheeler had collided with some motor homes. When they arrived on the scene, they realized the sheer magnitude of what they were facing. The fully-fueled plane had crash-landed into a lot of RVs, most of which had tanks full of fuel themselves.

The rescuers battled the fire, which now engulfed the plane, but in the end, they were helpless against the jet fuel powering the blaze. Many were distraught at not being able to do more.

George Kitchen, captain of the Reno Fire Department Station 6, arrived on the scene and got his crew ready to battle the blaze. He noticed the chair sitting in the middle of the road. He directed Mike Mooney, a firefighter, to see if anything was in it. After seeing the blaze, he likely felt that there was no chance of anyone surviving. Mike rushed to the chair and found George Jr. He was suffering from some burns, abrasions, and bruising. His injuries were so slight that he hadn't even lost consciousness.

He wouldn't be the only survivor who came from the wreck. George Sr. also managed to survive the initial impact but suffered serious head injuries. There was another survivor who was pulled from the wreckage by first responders. Robert Miggins may have survived the initial impact, but most of his body was covered in third-degree burns.

ACCIDENTAL OVERSIGHT: REASONS WHY FLIGHT 203 CRASHED SOON AFTER TAKEOFF

The problems with the plane hadn't started after takeoff, but rather when it was still on the ground. A ground team of 10 was in charge of getting the plane ready for its flight. They split into three groups. One group pumped fuel, another loaded baggage, and the last was in charge of connecting a hose to the air start system.

This system was used to help get the engines of the plane to turn on. Compressed air is pumped into the compression chamber, which leads to the rotation of the turbine. This would cause the engine to start. Attaching the hose was an automatic action to the ground crew and was completed without incident. The air start door under the leading edge of the right wing was opened, and the hose was attached before pressurized air was pumped into the chamber.

The first problem would arise after the four engines were going. The ground-handling supervisor tried to reach the pilots. For some reason, his headset had failed to work, so he started communicating with the pilots using hand signals. The pilots confirmed the change of communication. This was followed by a hand signal to start taxiing the plane into position. However, the hose to the right air start was still attached, and a crew member was struggling to get it disconnected. The supervisor noticed this and stopped the plane before he went over to help the ground crew. The hose was removed, and the door was closed. Unfortunately, because of the rush to get the plane airborne, the door was not sealed correctly, and it wasn't double-checked.

Once the plane took off, this door flapped open, creating the odd sounds that George Jr. had heard. This caused vibrations throughout the aircraft, as it was acting like a spoiler, causing air resistance which led to the interruption of an airflow across the right wing. Captain Allen D. Heasley, an experienced pilot with over 14,500 hours flying, felt that there were problems with the engines.

He had the engines set to maximum except takeoff (METO), a power setting that offers the highest thrust levels, usually reserved for takeoffs or go-rounds. He concluded that if he gave less power to the engines and the vibrations stopped, there'd be an issue with the engines. He lowered the power to the engine, but it had no improvement to the vibration they felt. Realizing that there was something seriously wrong, he'd made it known that he was returning to the airport to resolve it.

Unfortunately, the copilot, Kevin Charles Fieldsa, wasn't keeping an eye on the flight path or airspeed they were traveling at, and it was dangerously low. If they continued at this speed, it would cause the plane to stall and drop out of the sky. Eventually, the inevitable happened. The airspeed dropped below what the wings would use to produce lift. Even when engine power was increased, it was too late, and there wasn't enough thrust left. This caused the plane to crash about a minute after taking off.

The impact with the ground had caused the fuel tanks to be breached, which led to the explosion. George Jr. had narrowly escaped being engulfed by flames. He had somehow managed to remain upright after being thrown from the plane. His father wasn't so lucky, as he had landed on his head.

Many things had gone wrong, and no one was sure how it all happened. That was until the black boxes were found. Upon inspection, it was discovered that the flight data recorder hadn't recorded anything from the flight, as it had run out of foil more than 100 flight hours before the flight. This was an older recorder that relied on a foil spoil to record data. The pilots had failed to check this before their flight, which was against protocol, though this wasn't the only protocol that hadn't been followed.

The plane's weight and center of gravity were never calculated. This was proven by the random seating arrangement. When the NTSB calculated it during the investigation, it was found that the center of gravity was out of its limits. The start and taxi checklists weren't completed correctly, and there was no predeparture briefing from the cockpit voice recorder (CVR). It was determined that poor procedure was the result of the captain feeling rushed. After all, he thought the plane was behind schedule. This was because, when he and his crew had been picked up, the plane had already been an hour late.

There had been no CRM training at Galaxy Airways, as it wasn't a requirement. This only became a mandate in the 1990s. When the trouble started in the flight, Captain Allen had taken over the situation, as he had more experience. The copilot and the flight engineer, Mark Charles Freels, both of whom had less experience, just took orders and didn't take any initiative during the situation. By relying on one person to make all the decisions, it was only a matter of time before one mistake resulted in an accident.

This breakdown of CRM prevented cohesion between the pilots, causing them to not notice the warning signs of the airspeed being too low. It was determined that the stress of the situation may have prevented the pilots from identifying which problems should be resolved first and multi-tasking correctly.

The captain also failed to follow correct protocol when the vibrations were detected. The crew should have flown to a higher, safer altitude before attempting to lower the power of the engines. The plane could still have been saved if the thrust had been returned in a timely fashion once it was determined that the engines weren't the cause of the vibrations. Yet the pilots weren't the only contributing factor.

Issues with the air start door for Lockheed Electra went as far back as 1970, but this was rarely reported as pilots had no way to tell the FAA discreetly without fear of retribution. The supervisor responsible for the ground crew had never worked on a Lockheed Electra before, and therefore, failed to correctly secure the door. The ground crew member who struggled with the hose was from Reno Flying Services, who had not received all the training they were meant to. They only had on-the-job training and hadn't had their classroom training. The mistakes by the ground crew were caused by their routine being broken by the broken headset, and the early taxiing led to the door not being properly closed.

There were other findings by NTSB which eventually led to massive fines being paid by Galaxy Airlines. This resulted in the airline closing its doors in the late 80s.

EATEN ALIVE BY GUILT, REACHING OUT TO OTHERS

Sadly, George Sr. and Robert didn't survive their injuries. George Sr. would die on January 29 from massive head injuries. Robert would die a little later on February 4 from the extensive burn trauma he suffered. This left George Jr. as the sole survivor of Flight 203. There had been 16 other people who survived the impact, but the fire claimed their lives before anyone could reach them.

George Jr. was wracked with guilt. Everything reminded him of his father, and he reminded everyone in his small town about what had happened. Friends struggled to talk to him, while sympathy poured in from around the world from complete strangers. Despite all this, he managed to graduate high school soon after being released from the hospital and went to study at St. Thomas College. It didn't last.

On January 28, 1986, one week after the anniversary of Flight 203's crash, the space shuttle Challenger exploded. This sent the country into mourning once more, but it sent George into a deep depression. He started to withdraw mentally and eventually dropped out of college. He felt that he had been given a second chance at life, and he was wasting it. His grief was also being prolonged by the NTSB investigation and ongoing lawsuits against Galaxy Airlines. He couldn't get over his survivor's guilt as he couldn't get closure over what had happened.

As the years passed, he eventually returned to Reno—perhaps subconsciously wanting to be close to his father—got married (and eventually divorced), before having his daughter, Hannah. Even after all these years, he didn't like to talk about the accident. However, he still suffered from survivor's guilt and felt that it was difficult to talk to people as there were no others who were like him; a sole survivor.

He decided that he wanted to know if there *were* others like him. He started a Facebook group dedicated to sole survivors of plane crashes. Not all survivors took kindly to him wanting to talk about their darkest day, but there were a few who willingly communicated with him. He managed to find some solace that he was no longer alone. He came to realize that these accidents just happen sometimes. There wasn't always a reason why someone survived while someone else didn't.

Ky Dickens, a survivor of a horrific car accident herself, approached George Jr. about making a documentary about sole survivors of plane crashes. This was the start of *Sole Survivor*, which brought four survivors together to tell their tale. After seeing the documentary for himself, George finally felt the burden he had been carrying his whole life start to lift; after almost 30 years. Today, George Jr. still reaches out to survivors to be their rock during their time of need. Perhaps this is why he survived Flight 203.

BONUS CHAPTER: IMPROVING YOUR ODDS OF SURVIVING A PLANE CRASH

Each individual managed to survive in different ways, so what determines whether a crash is survivable or not? In essence, it comes down to three things: tolerance, structure, and the surrounding area. The body's tolerance (injury, forces on the body, etc.) is not exceeded, the structural integrity of the plane plays a large role, and the less the damage there is to the structure, the higher the chance of walking away from a crash. Then, after the crash, the surrounding area can also have an influence on the survival of those from the plane and those who rescue them. In inhospitable or dangerous areas, the chance of survival is lower. Even when a plane crash-lands in the water, as long as emergency services can get to the survivors quickly enough, there is a higher chance of surviving the ordeal.

THINGS TO CONSIDER

Although fatal plane crashes are rarer than fatal car crashes, they do still occur. While you can't do anything about an engine failure, you can improve your odds of surviving by what you wear and your actions.

Clothing

What you wear will be vital to your survival after a crash, as this will protect you from the environment. Long, tight-fitting, but comfortable clothing, made of cotton or other natural fibers, is the best to wear. Natural fibers are more resistant to burning and melting when coming into contact with fire. The longer clothing will protect your limbs from sharp objects and sitting tightly prevents it from snagging on items and slowing you down. Even by having a jacket with you, you can use it as a shield to prevent anything hot (melted plastic, fuel, etc.) from raining down on you. Sneakers or boots are your best footwear, as they offer more protection for your feet and will not easily fall off. High heels will be one of the first items you will have to discard, so choose your shoes carefully.

Remove sharp objects from your pockets, as these will cut you during a crash. Remove items such as scarves, ties, and glasses when told a crash landing is imminent. Items around your neck can choke you, while lost glasses make it difficult to navigate your way out of the plane.

Location

There is no single seat on a plane that will guarantee your survival in a crash. However, there are parts of the plane which are statistically safer than others. The tail-end of the plane is considered to have the highest chance of survival, while the middle has the least. After that, the middle seat is considered safer than those surrounding it. Being within five rows of an emergency exit is also preferable. The longer it takes you to leave a plane after a crash, the lower your chance of survival will be.

Safety Briefing

It cannot be stressed enough that you *need to listen* to the safety briefing. Whether it is your first or 300th time, you must listen to the safety instructions and be familiar with the safety pamphlet. Valuable information that could save your life is presented to you with every flight. Many people brush these instructions off, and it can have a detrimental effect if something were to go wrong. An example of this level of complacency was seen on November 23, 1996. Ethiopian Airlines Flight 961 was forced to make a water landing, resulting in the deaths of 125 out of the 175 people on board. It hadn't been the landing that killed them, but rather people inflating their life jackets while still inside the cabin. As the plane started taking on water, they were too buoyant to get out of the sinking plane and drowned.

Don't assume the safety instructions are the same for all planes. The moment you sit down in your seat, put on your seatbelt, read the safety pamphlet, and then listen to the instructions. They could one day save your life.

Learn to brace correctly. If you are unsure, ask the flight attendant to show you how. The idea behind the brace position is to protect your head and limbs from the sudden stop at the end of the crash. Injuries to the head are caused by striking the seat in front of you, while injuries to arms are caused by them flailing around. Loose limbs will break when they make contact with other objects around you. Don't interlock your fingers; rather, have your nondominant hand over your dominant one. This way, you can save at least one of your hands from damage.

Hand Luggage

Although it's easier to place all hand luggage in the baggage compartment above you, it's safer to keep it at your feet. In the event of an imminent crash, having this luggage under the seat in front of you prevents your legs and feet from going into that gap, potentially breaking or injuring them. It also assists you in curling into the fetal position when bracing.

Attitude

It is vital to have the right attitude when it comes to flying. Not every single bump or dip means that a crash is going to happen. Remaining calm and thinking of the future allows you to develop a positive outlook on life. Remember: plane crashes are *rare*.

After the Crash

Once the initial crash has been survived, don't start to celebrate. You will need to get out of the plane as quickly and as orderly as possible. Listen for any instructions. If none are forthcoming, do as you were instructed during the safety presentation—especially those at the emergency exits. Depending on the condition of the plane, you may need to move quite far (up to 500 feet or more) from it to prevent yourself from being caught up in a potential explosion. Don't worry about your luggage! Your dawdling can lower not only your chance of survival, but anyone else you are holding up. Only return to the body of the plane once it has been deemed safe to do so.

When a plane goes down, there are hundreds of people who scramble to come to the rescue. However, sometimes crashes are in remote or difficult to reach places. If this occurs, survivors may have to fend for themselves for an undetermined duration. This is when the rule of threes comes into play. Surviving the initial crash is fortunate, but to extend that good fortune, you will need to consider things required for your survival. This is shelter, water, and food. The rule of three explains how a person can succumb to exposure within three hours (depending on environmental conditions): three days without water and up to three weeks without food. However, this can vary depending on the condition of the survivors. Those who are injured may succumb easier than those who aren't.

Once the plane is deemed safe to return to, it is a treasure trove of items that can help with continued survival. Although it may be easier to strip a smaller and lighter plane than those used for commercial flight, it is possible to use various pieces of the aircraft. Anything on, in, or that has fallen off the plane will be useful to you. Don't be afraid to strip away what you need to stay alive. However, the condition of the plane will determine what you could use.

The aluminum skin of the aircraft can be used as a makeshift shelter, shovels, and even splints. Wires and cabling can act as cordage, which can be used to tie a variety of items together. This can even be used to make a tourniquet, if necessary. The wing and nose tips can make excellent holders to carry water, while the fabric from the seats can be used to filter it before drinking. Even the seatbelts can be used as bandages and slings. The list is extensive, so use your imagination. Don't forget to raid the first aid kit and the food carts to keep you going a little longer.

Work together as a team with other survivors, and all those with you will stand a better chance at overcoming your ordeal. Ask people about their survival skills. You'd be surprised what information some people may have up their sleeve.

Lastly, never leave the site of a crash. For the most part, rescue workers will know where you are and will arrive to help. Remain in the general vicinity, so it is easier to be found.

FINAL THOUGHTS

Many people have survived hardships in their past. They were able to get over those events by speaking to loved ones, people who have gone through what they have gone through, and even trained professionals. But what happens when you are part of a rare survivor's group, where only you survived out of perhaps hundreds? Surviving a plane crash is lucky enough, but when you are the only one, it can be pure torture.

When most people realize that they are talking to a survivor, their interaction is almost textbook. First, there is the amazement of their survival. This is followed shortly by pity, and finally, awkwardness. This is not what survivors want or need. They are as much victims as those buried after the accident, except that they have to live with the loss and guilt for the remainder of their days.

Most survivors suffer from survivor's guilt and likely PTSD from what they had to experience. They may even feel that they are being judged for being alive when so many others died. It is difficult for them to speak to people about what happened.

This was the case for many of the survivors discussed in this book. Often, they felt alone with their thoughts because there was no one else who could understand what they were forced to go through. Some even blame themselves for what happened, thinking they could have changed the end result. Sadly, this isn't possible.

Many are left with the always unanswered question: why me? Why did I live and so many others didn't make it? There are so many factors involved in whether a person survives a plane crash or not. It is difficult to point to one thing which will always save you. Survival of a plane crash is determined by whether your body can handle the strain placed on it, whether the structure of the plane holds after the impact, and if the surrounding area is safe enough to leave the wreckage behind.

There is no single, magical seat on all planes that will guarantee your safety. However, there are many ways you can improve your chances. Taking a middle seat within five rows of an exit and close to the back of the plane is a sure way to increase your odds. It is also a good idea to dress appropriately when flying. This can help to protect your body if you need to leave the plane quickly or if you have to survive in the area surrounding the crash site.

There is nothing to fear from flying. Although a plane crash is disturbing, it isn't an event that occurs frequently, and you are more likely to be in a car accident. As long as you abide by the safety instructions given to you by the cabin crew, you will have a higher chance at surviving in a commercial flight.

At the end of the day, overcoming any challenge comes down to you as an individual and maybe a little luck. If you are of sound mind and body, you can push yourself to your limits to achieve your goals and survive anything life has to throw at you.

REFERENCES

37000 Feet. (n.d.-a). *Flight crew of an medium large transport air carrier aircraft inadvertently taxied into position for takeoff on the wrong runway.* http://www.37000feet.com/report/256788

37000 Feet. (n.d.-b). *Lex controller described an attempt by an LJ45 flight crew to take off on the wrong runway as they turned onto runway 26 when runway 22 was issued.* http://www.37000feet.com/report/722668

ABS-CBN News. (2018, April 13). *Journalist Nestor Mata dies at 92.* https://news.abs-cbn.com/news/04/13/18/journalist-nestor-mata-dies-at-92?fbclid=IwAR3myM3i8TgPUVsOQcCrOVmACIRw3pLvv-_dS7CPreFewTfI7eUFr247EOg

Admin. (2020, January 28). *Part 121 vs. 135, 125 and 91 of FAA regulations.* AVISAV. https://avisav.com/2020/01/28/part-121-vs-135-125-and-91-of-faa-regulations/

Admiral Cloudberg. (2021, April 12). *Gambling with fate: The crash of Galaxy Airlines flight 203*. Medium. https://admiralcloudberg.medium.com/gambling-with-fate-the-crash-of-galaxy-airlines-flight-203-91f15c871055

Associated Press. (2006, September 25). *Family of co-pilot who survived Kentucky crash says he does not remember accident*. Deseret News. https://www.deseret.com/2006/9/25/19975965/family-of-co-pilot-who-survived-kentucky-crash-says-he-does-not-remember-accident

Associated Press. (2011, August 27). *Ky. plane crash victims remembered in sculpture*. Deseret News. https://www.deseret.com/2011/8/27/20212094/ky-plane-crash-victims-remembered-in-sculpture

Associated Press. (2015, March 25). *Surviving pilot had clean record until Ky. comair crash*. Fox News. https://www.foxnews.com/story/surviving-pilot-had-clean-record-until-ky-comair-crash

Aviation Pros. (2007, August 23). *Former tower chief defends controller*. https://www.aviationpros.com/home/news/10386380/former-tower-chief-defends-controller

Backcountry Chronicles. (n.d.). *Wilderness survival rules of 3 – air, shelter, water and food*. https://www.backcountrychronicles.com/wilderness-survival-rules-of-3/

Bakari, B., & Guendouz, O. (2010). *Moi Bahia, la miraculée*. Succès Du Livre, Dl.

Baum Hedlund. (n.d.). *Why planes crash*. https://www.baumhedlundlaw.com/aviation-accident/why-planes-crash/

BBC News. (2010, May 13). *Are children more likely to survive plane crashes?* http://news.bbc.co.uk/2/hi/uk_news/magazine/8679572.stm

BBC News. (2012, March 24). *Juliane Koepcke: How I survived a plane crash.* https://www.bbc.com/news/magazine-17476615

BBC News. (2015a, June 25). *Miraculous plane crash survivors.* https://www.bbc.com/news/world-latin-america-33268614

BBC News. (2015b, June 26). *Mother and baby survive Colombia jungle plane crash.* https://www.bbc.com/news/world-latin-america-33265943

BBC News. (2016, December 24). *Vesna Vulovic, stewardess who survived 33,000ft fall, dies.* https://www.bbc.com/news/world-europe-38427411

BBC News. (2018, August 1). *How likely are you to survive a plane crash?* https://www.bbc.com/news/world-45030345

Bennetto, J. (1993, August 8). *Inquiry demanded after air crash bodies are sent to wrong families:* The Independent. https://www.independent.co.uk/news/uk/inquiry-demanded-after-air-crash-bodies-are-sent-to-wrong-families-just-what-did-happen-after-flight-vn474-from-ho-chi-minh-city-hit-a-mountain-in-bad-weather-jason-bennetto-reports-1460019.html

Bilefsky, D. (2008, April 26). *Serbia's most famous survivor fears that recent history will repeat itself.* The New York Times. https://www.nytimes.com/2008/04/26/world/europe/26vulovic.html?action=click&module=RelatedCoverage&pgtype=Article®ion=Footer

Bogdanowicz, O. (2021, January 7). *The only survivor of LANSA 508.* Medium. https://historyofyesterday.com/the-only-survivor-of-lansa-508-5a222a21d255

Bowden, G. H. (1986, January 21). *Families of plane crash victims grieving year after tragedy.* AP News. https://apnews.com/article/cecfbd543ed674a2cc78a3b2d932da53

Boyle, L. (2012, August 14). *"When I look in mirror, I have visual scars": Sole survivor of 1987 Michigan plane crash speaks for first time about disaster in which 156 people - including her family - died.* Mail Online. https://www.dailymail.co.uk/news/article-2188168/Sole-survivor-Michigan-plane-crash-1987-Cecelia-Cichan-speaks-time-25-years.html

Bureau of Aircraft Accidents Archives. (n.d.-a). *Accident archives.* https://www.baaa-acro.com/crash-archives

Bureau of Aircraft Accidents Archives. (n.d.-b). *Accidents rate per year.* Retrieved March 4, 2022, from https://www.baaa-acro.com/statistics/crashs-rate-per-year

Bureau of Aircraft Accidents Archives. (n.d.-c). *Death rate per year.* https://www.baaa-acro.com/statistics/death-rate-per-year

Cavus, A. (2018, July 1). *Juliane Diller.* Panguana. https://panguana.de/about-us/juliane-diller/?lang=en

CBC Radio. (2016, December 28). *Remembering Vesna Vulović, flight attendant who survived 10,000-metre fall from plane.* https://www.cbc.ca/radio/asithappens/as-it-happens-wednesday-edition-1.3914159/remembering-vesna-vulovi%C4%87-flight-attendant-who-survived-10-000-metre-fall-from-plane-1.3914164

CBS News. (2006, October 3). *Comair crash survivor leaves hospital.* https://www.cbsnews.com/news/comair-crash-survivor-leaves-hospital/

CBS News. (2009, July 15). *Teen Bahia Bakari battered, bruised after surviving Yemenia Airlines plane crash near Comoros island.* Web Archive. https://web.archive.org/web/20090715230326/http://cbs5.com/national/yemenia.plane.crash.2.1066879.html

CBS News. (2010, May 13). *Libyan crash survivor reunites with relatives.* https://www.cbsnews.com/news/libyan-crash-survivor-reunites-with-relatives/

Cherry, K. (2021, February 20). *What is survivor's guilt?* Verywell Mind. https://www.verywellmind.com/survivors-guilt-4688743

Clark, A. (2016, January 9). *The LANSA Flight 508 crash: Juliane Koepcke and 11 days of survival.* Disciples of Flight. https://disciplesofflight.com/the-lansa-flight-508-crash-juliane-koepcke/

Clifton, G. (2015, January 20). *Memories still raw for sole survivor of '85 plane crash.* USA Today. https://www.usatoday.com/story/news/nation/2015/01/20/memories-still-raw-for-sole-survivor-of-85-plane-crash/22080969/

CNN Editorial Research. (2022, February 17). *Commercial passenger airplane crashes fast facts.* CNN. https://edition.cnn.com/2013/07/09/world/commercial-passenger-airplane-crashes-fast-facts/index.html

CNN. (2009, July 2). *"Miracle" plane crash survivor back in France.* http://edition.cnn.com/2009/WORLD/europe/07/02/yemen.plane.survivor/

CNN. (2014, January 18). *I was the sole survivor: 4 stories of plane crash survival.* https://edition.cnn.com/interactive/2014/01/world/sole-survivor/

CNN. (n.d.). *Co-pilot survived crash that killed 49.* https://edition.cnn.com/videos/bestoftv/2014/01/06/sole-survivor-jim.cnn

Connolly, K. (2009, January 13). *Woman who fell to earth: Was air crash survivor's record just propaganda?* The Guardian. https://www.theguardian.com/world/2009/jan/13/flight-attendant-record-fall-hoax

Deutsche Welle. (2020, September 1). *How does a black box work?* https://www.dw.com/en/how-does-a-black-box-work/a-17907283

Doddridge, R. (2017). *Is it better to go loose or tense up before impact?* Quora. https://www.quora.com/Is-it-better-to-go-loose-or-tense-up-before-impact

Editors. (n.d.). *Juliane Koepcke biography.* The Famous People. https://www.thefamouspeople.com/profiles/juliane-koepcke-34275.php

Elgot, J., Kassam, A., & Brodzinsky, S. (2015, June 25). *Mother left trail for rescuers to find her and baby after Colombian plane crash.* The Guardian. https://www.theguardian.com/world/2015/jun/25/colombia-plane-crash-rescue-mother-baby

Eveleth, R. (2013, August 27). *The curse of being a sole survivor.* Nautilus. https://nautil.us/the-curse-of-being-a-sole-survivor-994/

Fleming, E. (2019, June 12). *How did Nestor Mata survive?* Sidmartin Bio. https://www.sidmartinbio.org/how-did-nestor-mata-survive/

Galarpe, K. (2018, June 3). *Remembering my editor, Mr. Nestor Mata.* GMA News Online. https://www.gmanetwork.com/news/lifestyle/familyandrelationships/655552/remembering-my-editor-mr-nestor-mata/story/

Godfrey, K. (2021, September 7). *The best ways to increase your odds of surviving a plane crash including what to wear and which seats to avoid.* The Sun. https://www.thesun.co.uk/travel/16071383/how-to-survive-plane-crash-wear-best-seat/

Goldberg, M. (2016, May 27). *First responders tell us why drunk people are more likely to survive a collision.* The Drive. https://www.thedrive.com/news/3704/first-responders-tell-us-why-drunk-people-are-more-likely-to-survive-a-collision

Goldfarb, K. (2018, April 13). *The incredible story of Juliane Koepcke, the teenager who fell 10,000 feet and trekked the jungle for 11 days.* All That's Interesting. https://allthatsinteresting.com/juliane-koepcke

Golgowski, N. (2014, January 7). *Lone teen survivor, Bahia Bakari, of Indian Ocean plane crash that killed 152 recalls survival.* New York Daily News. https://www.nydailynews.com/news/world/lone-survivor-plane-recalls-survival-sea-article-1.1569132

Gulf News. (2006, September 8). *Sole plane crash survivor asks "why did God do this to me?"* https://gulfnews.com/world/americas/sole-plane-crash-survivor-asks-why-did-god-do-this-to-me-1.254234

Haddad, K. (2021, August 16). *34 years ago: Northwest Flight 255 crashes after takeoff from Detroit Metro Airport.* Click on Detroit. https://www.clickondetroit.com/all-about-michigan/2019/08/15/32-years-ago-northwest-flight-255-crashes-after-takeoff-from-detroit-metro-airport/

Halladay, J. (2013, July 19). *"Sole Survivor" film gives comair crash families pause.* USA Today. https://www.usatoday.com/story/news/nation/2013/07/19/sole-survivor-film-gives-comair-crash-families-pause/2567507/

Harvey-Jenner, C. (2016, October 3). *This woman was the only survivor of a plane crash and had to spend 8 days alone in a Vietnam jungle.* Cosmopolitan. https://www.cosmopolitan.com/uk/reports/news/a46317/annette-herfkens-only-survivor-plane-crash-vietnam-jungle/

IMDb. (2013, November 13). *Sole survivor.* https://www.imdb.com/title/tt1966575/

Korman, R. (2017, June 14). *Are some airlines just too dangerous to fly?* Pacific Standard. https://psmag.com/economics/are-some-airlines-just-too-dangerous-to-fly-3460

KSTP. (2020). *Flashback friday: Minnesota man sole survivor of Galaxy Airlines crash 35 years ago* [Video]. YouTube. https://www.youtube.com/watch?v=cUoyN_iDCJM

Lamson, G. Jr. (2014, January 10). *Helping fellow plane crash survivors has changed my life.* CNN. https://edition.cnn.com/2014/01/08/opinion/sole-survivor-george-lamson/index.html

Learmount, D. (2022, January 1). *Airline accident fatalities in 2021 more than halved from previous year.* Flight Global. https://www.flightglobal.com/airlines/airline-accident-fatalities-in-2021-more-than-halved-from-previous-year/146990.article

Leff, G. (2019, November 14). *Vietnam Airlines Flight 474 had 1 survivor who lived 8 days in the jungle.* View from the Wing. https://viewfromthewing.com/sole-survivor-of-vietnam-airlines-flight-474-crash-lived-8-days-in-the-jungle/

Lesser Lesser Landy & Smith PLLC. (2021, June 23). *Is flying safer than driving?* https://www.lesserlawfirm.com/is-flying-safer-than-driving/

Levy, M. (2014, March 21). *Malaysia Airlines search: how Bahia Bakari proved miracles do happen.* The Sydney Morning Herald. https://www.smh.com.au/world/malaysia-airlines-search-how-bahia-bakari-proved-miracles-do-happen-20140321-hvl84.html

Libyan Civil Aviation Authority. (2013, February). *Final report of Afriqiyah airways aircraft Airbus A330-202, 5A-ONG crash occurred at Tripoli (Libya) on 12/05/2010.* Wayback Machine. https://web.archive.org/web/20130903094253/http:/caa.ly/finalReport/FINAL_5A-ONG-1.pdf

McCarthy, E. (2007, January 17). *Comair pilot called deadly airstrip "weird": Crash update.* Popular Mechanics. https://www.popularmechanics.com/flight/a1264/4212159/

McMah, L. (2019, May 25). *The sole survivor of a plane crash and her 192 hours alone in the jungle.* NZ Herald. https://www.nzherald.co.nz/world/the-sole-survivor-of-vietnam-airlines-flight-474-and-her-192-hours-alone-in-the-jungle/HMZVPKVBCAC5AKDUYX4FV4RDFQ/

McMurray, J. (2018, October 17). *NTSB says pilot error caused Kentucky plane crash.* Rutland Herald. https://www.rutlandherald.com/news/ntsb-says-pilot-error-caused-kentucky-plane-crash/article_3100e9c6-004c-571f-8c9c-fc5cf231e932.html

Meikle, J., & agencies. (2010, May 14). *Blog details Libya plane crash survivor's safari with family.* The Guardian. https://www.theguardian.com/world/2010/may/14/blog-libya-plane-crash-survivor

National Aeronautics and Space Administration. (n.d.). *Flaps and slats.* Retrieved February 24, 2022, from https://www.grc.nasa.gov/www/k-12/airplane/flap.html

National Transportation Safety Board. (1986, February 4). *Aircraft accident report: Galaxy Airlines, inc., Lockheed Electra-L-188C, N5532 Reno, Nevada January 21, 1985.* Embry-Riddle Aeronautical University. http://libraryonline.erau.edu/online-full-text/ntsb/aircraft-accident-reports/AAR86-01.pdf

National Transportation Safety Board. (2007). *Attempted takeoff from wrong runway Comair Flight 5191 Bombardier CL-600-2B19, N431CA Lexington, Kentucky August 27, 2006.* https://reports.aviation-safety.net/2006/20060827-0_CRJ1_N431CA.pdf

NBC News. (2010, May 14). *Dutch crash survivor learns of family's death.* https://www.nbcnews.com/id/wbna37145872

Newdick, T. (2022, January 26). *An air stewardess fell 33,000 feet and lived to tell the tale 50 years ago today.* The Drive. https://www.thedrive.com/the-war-zone/44038/an-air-stewardess-fell-33000-feet-and-lived-to-tell-the-tale-60-years-ago-today

News Wires. (2010, May 15). *Dutch child survivor of Tripoli airplane crash returns home.* France 24. https://www.france24.com/en/20100515-child-survivor-airplane-crash-returns-home-libya-netherlands

News24. (2015, June 26). *Colombia "miracle" mom's tremendous fight to save baby.* https://www.news24.com/news24/colombia-miracle-moms-tremendous-fight-to-save-baby-20150626

Ocampo, A. R. (2018, April 27). *Mata, the lone survivor.* Inquirer.Net. https://opinion.inquirer.net/112754/mata-lone-survivor

Outlook-BBC Sounds. (2012, March 20). *The woman who fell from the sky: The aircrash sole-survivor's story.* https://www.bbc.co.uk/sounds/play/p00pkc3y

Owl Apps. (n.d.). *1957 Cebu Douglas C-47 crash.* http://next.owlapps.net/owlapps_apps/article?id=16453055&lang=en

Page, C. (2020, January 11). *What's happens on during a go-around before landing?* The Points Guy. https://thepointsguy.com/guide/what-happens-during-go-around/

Paramount Business Jets. (n.d.). *Instrument meteorological conditions.* https://www.paramountbusinessjets.com/aviation-terminology/instrument-meteorological-conditions.html

Patrick. (2010, May 10). *het dagboek....* http://onsgaanopvakansie.blogspot.com/2010/05/het-dagboek.html

Pearson, N. (2018, November 3). *Juliane Koepcke: The girl who fell 3km from a plane explosion and survived.* 9News. https://www.9news.com.au/world/juliane-koepcke-german-teen-plane-explosion-survivor-peru-amazon-jungle-survival-story/8d5ea207-6dd3-4a88-9d18-a52194566cb0

Pearson, N. (2019, October 4). *Vesna Vulovic: The flight attendant who fell 10km in a plane bombing and survived.* 9 News. https://www.9news.com.au/world/vesna-vulovic-flight-attendant--fell-10km-plane-bombing-survival-no-parachute-serbia-news/7a369341-a6f1-41b5-9a66-9bf6dd9ffb34

Penguin Random House. (2019, November 22). *A conversation with Ann Napolitano, author of Dear Edward.* Library Journal. https://www.libraryjournal.com/story/a-conversation-with-ann-napolitano-author-of-dear-edward?page=register

Perez, A., & Fies, A. (2013, May 17). *Cecelia Crocker, other plane crash "Sole Survivors" share tales of guilt, pain and triumph.* ABC News. https://abcnews.go.com/US/cecelia-crocker-plane-crash-sole-survivors-share-tales/story?id=19198107

Peterson, B. (1987, August 21). *4-Year-old Cecilia awakens, asks for mother, then doll.* The Washington Post. https://www.washingtonpost.com/archive/politics/1987/08/21/4-year-old-cecilia-awakens-asks-for-mother-then-doll/24aa7ebb-f282-42b0-b501-de8aff61264a/

Pew, G. (2012, May 17). *James Polehinke, sole survivor.* AVweb. https://www.avweb.com/news/james-polehinke-sole-survivor/

Pinkerton, P. (2016, December 16). *Surviving a plane crash pt3 - using aircraft parts in survival.* Outdoor Revival. https://www.outdoorrevival.com/instant-articles/surviving-plane-crash-pt3-using-aircraft-parts-survival.html?firefox=1

R.G.J. archives. (2021, January 21). *Jan. 21, 1985: Galaxy Airlines Flight 203 crashes into field at South Virginia and Neil.* Reno Gazette Journal. https://www.rgj.com/story/news/2020/01/21/jan-21-1985-charter-flight-crashes-into-reno-field/4536527002/

Radford, B. (2010, May 13). *What's an air pocket?* Live Science. https://www.livescience.com/32586-what-is-an-air-pocket.html

Ranter, H. (2019). *ASN aircraft accident Canadair CL-600-2B19 Regional Jet CRJ-100ER N431CA Lexington-Blue Grass Airport, KY (LEX)*. Aviation Safety Network. https://aviation-safety.net/database/record.php?id=20060827-0

Ranter, H. (n.d.-a). *[ASN Aircraft accident Yakovlev Yak-40 VN-A449 Son Trung]*. Aviation Safety Network. https://aviation-safety.net/database/record.php?id=19921114-1

Ranter, H. (n.d.-b). [Accident Cessna T303 Crusader HK-4677G, 20 Jun 2015.] Aviation Safety Network. https://aviation-safety.net/wikibase/177138

Ranter, H. (n.d.-c). *[ASN aircraft accident Airbus A330-202 5A-ONG Tripoli International Airport (TIP)]*. Aviation Safety Network. https://aviation-safety.net/database/record.php?id=20100512-0

Ranter, H. (n.d.-d). *[ASN Aircraft accident Douglas C-47A-75-DL (DC-3) 2100925 Cebu]*. Aviation Safety Network. https://aviation-safety.net/database/record.php?id=19570317-0

Ridley, J. (2016, October 2). *I was the sole survivor of a plane crash -- and spent 8 days in the jungle.* New York Post. https://nypost.com/2016/10/02/i-was-the-sole-survivor-of-a-plane-crash-and-spent-7-days-in-the-jungle/

Romo, R. (2015, June 25). *Colombian plane crash: Mother, baby survive in jungle.* CNN. https://edition.cnn.com/2015/06/25/world/colombian-mother-infant-plane-crash/index.html

Salsa, R. (2020, August 26). *How to survive A plane crash.* Lessons from History. https://medium.com/lessons-from-history/how-to-survive-a-plane-crash-491d4e18906f

Sandomir, R. (2016, December 28). *Vesna Vulovic, flight attendant who survived jetliner blast, dies at 66.* The New York Times. https://www.nytimes.com/2016/12/28/world/europe/vesna-vulovic-died-flight-attendant-in-plunge.html

Semch44. (2012). *Northwest Flight 255 news coverage - Detroit* [Video]. YouTube. https://www.youtube.com/watch?v=mBMUZ2YlAVo

Sharp, T. (2018, May 22). *World's first commercial airline.* Space. https://www.space.com/16657-worlds-first-commercial-airline-the-greatest-moments-in-flight.html

Shih, C., Lourenco, L., Van Dommelen, L., & Krothapalli, A. (1992). Unsteady flow past an airfoil pitching at a constant rate. *AIAA Journal, 30*(5), 1153–1161. https://doi.org/10.2514/3.11045

Smith, J. (2016, October 2). *Sole survivor of Vietnam plane crash which killed 29 people tells how she clung to life in the jungle for a week with fractured hips, gangrene and bone sticking out of her shin.* Mail Online. https://www.dailymail.co.uk/news/article-3818205/Sole-survivor-Vietnam-plane-crash-killed-29-people-tells-clung-life-jungle-WEEK-fractured-hips-gangrene-BONE-sticking-shin.html

Sowry, M. (2006, August 29). *Survivor in a plane crash that killed 49.* ABC News. https://abcnews.go.com/US/story?id=2367566&page=1

Staff and agencies. (2010, May 16). *Libya plane crash survivor flies home.* The Guardian. https://www.theguardian.com/world/2010/may/16/libya-plane-crash-survivor-home

Staff and agencies. (2016, December 24). *Serbian survivor of fall from plane explosion dies at 66.* The Guardian. https://www.theguardian.com/world/2016/dec/24/vesna-vulovic-serbian-survivor-of-fall-from-plane-explosion-dies-at-66

Sullivan, B. P. T. (2014, January 9). *Documentary that features Flight 5191 co-pilot to air on CNN Thursday.* The Courier-Journal. https://www.courier-journal.com/story/news/local/2014/01/09/documentary-that-features-flight-5191-co-pilot-to-air-on-cnn-thursday/4396789/

Tan, A. (2015, June 25). *Mother and baby rescued after surviving 5 days in Colombian jungle following plane crash.* ABC News. https://abcnews.go.com/International/mother-baby-rescued-surviving-days-colombian-jungle-plane/story?id=32028463

Tang, A., & Huang, M. Y. (2020, February 4). *Airplane accidents are 95% survivable. Here are seven ways to increase those odds even more.* Business Insider. https://www.businessinsider.com/seven-ways-increase-your-odds-surviving-plane-crash-2020-1?IR=T

Tempo Online. (2017, March 20). *Remembering President Ramon Magsaysay.* https://www.tempo.com.ph/2017/03/20/remembering-president-ramon-magsaysay/

The Associated Press. (2007, January 17). *Airline: Pilots in crash discussed family, jobs.* NBC News. https://www.nbcnews.com/id/wbna16671549

The Associated Press. (2019, January 10). *Lone survivor of 1987 plane crash, then 4, tells her story 26 years later.* Oregon Live. https://www.oregonlive.com/movies/2013/05/lone_survivor_of_1987_plane_cr.html

Thompson, H. (2014, July 8). *14 Fun Facts About Piranhas.* Smithsonian Magazine. https://www.smithsonianmag.com/science-nature/14-fun-facts-about-piranhas-180951948/

Ty, L. O. (1957, April 6). *Nestor Mata's story, April 6, 1957.* The Philippines Free Press Online. https://philippinesfreepress.wordpress.com/1957/04/06/nestor-matas-story-april-6-1957/

U.S. News. (2015, June 25). *Miracle: Mom and baby survive plane crash.* https://www.usnews.com/news/world/articles/2015/06/25/mother-baby-rescued-4-days-after-colombia-plane-crash?src=usn_Fb&fbclid=IwAR1GVKuZq_ir44eAkBHfvuBUakA6usDbuFEVKZqqfNVy_oT3p1hxwZfw4AQ

United Nations News. (2021, December 3). *With 1.3 million annual road deaths, UN wants to halve number by 2030.* https://news.un.org/en/story/2021/12/1107152

Vnuk, H. (2019, July 26). *Annette Herfkens was the sole survivor of a plane crash. Her fiancé died beside her.* Mamamia. https://www.mamamia.com.au/annette-herfkens/

Wade-Palmer, C. (2021, June 30). *"Miracle girl" only survivor of plane crash after 14 hours alone at sea.* Dailystar. https://www.dailystar.co.uk/news/world-news/miracle-girl-only-survivor-plane-24428235

Watkins, M. (2016, August 26). *Comair crash 10 years later: Things to know.* The Courier-Journal. https://www.courier-journal.com/story/news/local/2016/08/25/comair-crash-10-years-later-things-know/89303928/

Wave. (2006, September 15). *Doctor: Lone survivor of plane crash will recover from injuries.* https://www.wave3.com/story/5383049/doctor-lone-survivor-of-plane-crash-will-recover-from-injuries/

Wells, K. (2013, May 17). *Families of Flight 255 victims wait 26 years to hear sole survivor speak.* Michigan Radio. https://www.michiganradio.org/arts-culture/2013-05-17/families-of-flight-255-victims-wait-26-years-to-hear-sole-survivor-speak

Whittaker, F. (2015, June 25). *A mom and her baby survived for five days in the jungle after a plane crash.* BuzzFeed News. https://www.buzzfeednews.com/article/franciswhittaker/mother-and-baby-survive-plane-crash-in-colombia

Wise, J. (2016, April 16). *The gift and the guilt of the sole survivor.* Reader's Digest. https://www.rd.com/article/sole-survivor/

WYMT News Staff. (2019, August 28). *13 years ago today, Comair Flight 5191 kills 49 in Lexington.* https://www.wymt.com/content/news/13-years-ago-Comair-Flight-5191-kills-49-in-Lexington-558485501.html

Yahoo!News. (2012, November 18). *Nestor Mata: After falling from heaven, a passionate life of music, journalism, chess, and art.* https://ph.news.yahoo.com/nestor-mata-falling-heaven-passionate-life-music-journalism-081126839.html

ABOUT THE AUTHOR

When I am not busy "exploring our backyard" and admiring the endless beauty of New Zealand with my family, I like to write and share other people's personal stories of survival and triumphs. With 13 years of working in health care as a nurse under my belt, I have grown to connect with people I have worked with along the way. Witnessing their struggles, I have learned to appreciate how people survive and thrive even in their worst. My father, who was a survivor himself of a maritime disaster is an inspiration to my journey in writing and sharing these unbelievable and inspiring stories.

Come, and join me as I share with you amazing stories of people struck by disaster, and how they have seemingly survived the unsurvivable. And explore how you too can improve your odds in a similar situation.

Made in United States
North Haven, CT
20 August 2022